Echoes of Voidness

Geshé Rabten

Translated and edited
by Stephen Batchelor

Wisdom Publications · London

First published in 1983

Wisdom Publications
291 Brompton Road
London SW3 2DY
England

© Geshé Rabten and
Stephen Batchelor 1983

ISBN 0 86171 010 x

Illustrations on pages 14, 46 & 92
by Andy Weber

Typeset in Plantin 11 on 13 point
by Setrite and printed and bound
by J. Helen Productions, Hong Kong

Contents

Introduction

The aim of this book is to present three principal stages in the understanding of the Buddhist concept of voidness (*shūnyatā*) as expressed in three distinct forms of Mahāyāna Buddhist literature. The first part of the book, the *Heart of Wisdom*, represents the Buddha's own formulation of this key concept as expressed in the *Perfection of Wisdom Sutras*. According to Tibetan tradition — contested by modern scholarship — this important discourse can be dated approximately 500 years before the Christian era. Irrespective of academic speculations concerning its origins, the major function of this sutra is to provide an authoritative pronouncement on the profound subject of voidness that can appeal to the non-rational, devotional elements of religious consciousness. In it, personifications of the optimum state of being — the Buddha himself and Avalokiteshvara — act and speak in a recognizable geographical and historical setting, thereby establishing a concrete focus for human faith. Not once in the discourse does the main speaker, Avalokiteshvara, attempt to appeal to the listeners' reason by putting forth any logical proofs for voidness. He simply arises from his meditation and spontaneously speaks from his heart, from his own direct experience of ultimate reality.

In this respect the *Heart of Wisdom* — and other such sutras — provide a firm basis of confidence and devotion upon which subsequent logical and philosophical considerations of voidness can be founded. Buddhist teachers have always stressed that to avoid the pitfall of dry intellectualization all such metaphysical considerations should arise out of a spiritual experience rooted in faith. Seen in this way, the so-called negative dialectic of Mādhyamaka philosophy, which later arose to clarify these wisdom sutras, ceases to be a mere development in the history of ideas and can be seen instead as performing a definite spiritual function. The operation of the dialectic itself is viewed as an essential movement in religious consciousness necessary for achieving the goal of spiritual life, the full awakening of buddhahood. To appreciate fully the Mādhyamaka philosophy of voidness, it is important never to lose sight of the role it plays in fulfilling the deepest concerns of the person applying its dialectical method.

The Mādhyamaka (lit.: the central or middle) philosophy is represented in the second part of our book. The specific work chosen is the sixth chapter of Chandrakīrti's *Guide to the Middle Way*, which we can date in approximately the sixth century of the Christian era. The Mādhyamaka as a distinct movement in Buddhist thought was originally expounded in the second century by the Indian sage Nāgārjuna, primarily in his *Fundamental Stanzas on the Middle Way*. This and his other major works on the subject of voidness are concise and cryptic. Their closely reasoned arguments are principally aimed at uprooting the deep-seated tendency of the human mind to ascribe a certain concrete, inherent self-existence to phenomena, independent of all conditioning factors. As the objects of his analysis Nāgārjuna takes such common notions as cause and effect, coming and going, the sense organs and so forth, and shows how the ordinary, unenlightened conception of such things is permeated by this mistaken belief in self-existence. Chandrakīrti's *Guide*, composed as a commentary to Nāgārjuna's *Fundamental Stanzas* some four hundred years later, uses the same dialectical method. But here he uses it primarily to refute specific philosophical viewpoints that intellectually affirm, either explicit or implicity, this pervasive but false idea of inherent existence.

In his *Guide*, therefore, Chandrakīrti puts Nāgārjuna's method to work in the arena of philosophical inquiry of sixth century India. He applies the Mādhyamaka critique not only to such traditional subjects as the views of a permanent self, but also to those fellow Buddhist philosophies that he considers have succumbed to the mistaken tendency of grasping at inherent existence. In sharp contrast to the *Heart of Wisdom*, his is an exposition of voidness — the absence of inherent existence — that addresses itself almost entirely to rational and intellectual faculties. Rarely does Chandrakīrti appeal to his readers' faith in or devotion to the Buddha to strengthen his position. The central thrust of his polemic is purely logical.

The *Heart of Wisdom* and the *Guide to the Middle Way* represent two poles in the religious consciousness concerning voidness, the ultimate nature of reality. The former is inspirational in character and evokes a non-rational, devotional appreciation while the latter is logical and stimulates a rational, analytical appreciation. For one's spiritual development to be complete, however, both aspects must interpenetrate and complement one another. Finally, they must be integrated in one's own meditational experience.

This meditative approach to the understanding of voidness is contained in the third part of the book, *Mahāmudrā*. In this section the methods of gaining a living experience of voidness are described. It places great emphasis on the necessity of first preparing the mind in such a way that it is most receptive to developing a direct intuition of the meaning of voidness. Such receptivity is primarily composed of three elements: purity, devotion and absorption. These three form the underlying matrix in the depths of which the analytic function of reason needs to be securely grounded. This state of consciousness is compared to a calm still lake in whose depths darts a tiny fish. Only in a carefully prepared and calmed mind can the intellectual dexterity induced by the Mādhyamaka dialectic penetrate and influence the entire range of a person's being. Thus this third presentation of voidness is, in many respects, a synthesis of the two earlier approaches. As such, mahāmudrā is experiential in character and elicits an existential appreciation of voidness.

The experience of mahāmudrā is as old as Buddhism itself. However, its explicit formulation as a distinct element in the religious consciousness of voidness can be traced only from the time of Saraha in about the first or second century. Initially the concept of mahāmudrā was associated solely with the tantric traditions of the mahāsiddhas, certain highly accomplished meditators of India. These early siddhas embodied to a large extent a reaction against contemporary trends of speculative metaphysics. For this reason the term mahāmudrā carried the connotation of an experiential rather than a logical appreciation of reality. It was probably only as the sutra and tantra traditions began to converge and unify once they were established in Tibet that the term mahāmudrā began to be used in the context of the sutra as well as the tantra practices.

The unification of sutra and tantra was one of the principal aims of Tsong Khapa (1357-1419), the founder of the Gelug lineage of Tibetan Buddhism. And it is on the basis of his oral teachings that the first Panchen Lama, Chökyi Gyaltsen (1570-1662), composed the *Root Text for the Gelugpa Oral Tradition of Mahāmudrā* and its auto-commentary, the sources for the presentation of mahāmudrā found in this book. In the Panchen Lama's texts mahāmudrā practice is clearly understood as the practical, existential component of voidness realization in both the sutra and tantra traditions.

Despite their different approaches to the subject of voidness, the three sections of this book are brought into unity through a consistent application of the interpretation of Tsong Khapa. In his explanations of voidness Tsong Khapa lays great emphasis on the importance of distinguishing precisely between the two truths: conventional and ultimate. He maintains that before proceeding with the negative mādhyamaka dialectic, in which all wrong views are refuted, it is essential to recognize that conventionally empirical phenomena do exist, that conventionally they bear defining characteristics and that conventionally they function according to the infallible laws of cause and effect. If the reality of

these phenomena is not clearly affirmed, there is the great danger
that an over-enthusiastic application of the dialectic may reject too
much, including the ethical basis — derived from understanding
the workings of cause and effect — upon which a correct understanding of voidness must be founded. In naively and prematurely
considering everything to be "void" — wrongly understood to
mean "non-existent" — one is liable to deny even the validity of
what does exist and function.

As Tsong Khapa stresses repeatedly, a genuine understanding
of voidness, far from undermining reality, is the only way one can
gain correct knowledge of the way in which empirical phenomena
do exist and function. In the final analysis, these two truths — the
ultimate truth of voidness and the conventional truth of empirical
phenomena — do not contradict but rather complement one
another. Phenomena are able to function effectively in causal
interrelationships precisely because by their very nature they are
void of any inherent self-existence. Conversely, the fact that they
are in essence void is most strikingly indicated by the fact that
their occurrence is invariably dependent upon causes, conditions,
component parts and mental imputation. This assertion echoes
the thought of Nāgārjuna when he declared in his *Fundamental
Stanzas* (XXIV.19):

> Because there are no phenomena which are not
> dependent arisings, there are no phenomena which are
> not void.

Therefore, voidness is not a transcendent absolute that is realized
through a total negation of the empirical world. Rather, it completely pervades all that is.

In addition to stressing the reality of the empirical world and the
validity of its laws, another important feature of Tsong Khapa's
presentation is his emphasis on the need to recognize clearly and
precisely what is negated by the concept of voidness. When
understanding voidness, exactly what is it that one realizes to be
void? Without having answered this question it is difficult to see
how the notion of voidness can have any real significance.

According to the thought of Tsong Khapa voidness means the
voidness of inherent existence. What are the characteristics that

distinguish this so-called inherent existence from mere existence? Most fundamentally it is that inherent existence is, in fact, totally imaginary and non-existent. To exist inherently would mean to exist independently of any and all conditioning factors. For example, an inherently existent table would be one that somehow exists entirely from the side of its own intrinsic, essential nature. It would be something that stands out all by itself, as though its causes, its parts and its being conventionally apprehended as a table all had nothing to do with its essential being. It is rather easy to recognize intellectually that such a mode of existence is a logical impossibility; nevertheless, we instinctively apprehend all phenomena — including ourselves — as existing in exactly this impossible manner. It is this mistaken apprehension of inherent existence that constitutes our ignorance (Skt. *avidyā*; literally, unknowing) and this ignorance, in turn, is the basis of all disturbing states of mind and all the mistaken and suffering-producing modes of behaviour that proceed from them.

Therefore, in order to be free from the distorted, disturbing and inauthentic aspects of our existence, we need to dispel their root cause: our ignorance. This means we must simply stop apprehending phenomena as though they inherently existed. But implied here is the necessity of recognizing this mode of apprehension and, in particular, the way in which it causes things to appear as though they inherently existed. Thus the first and in many respects the most important step is to discern clearly how the supposed quality of inherent existence appears to the mind. Only when we have an accurate conception of inherent existence can we possibly proceed to consider whether it actually exists or whether it is something we have merely imagined.

This emphasis on the importance of recognizing clearly what inherent existence signifies likewise aids us in further delineating the two truths. The basic formula here is the following. The ultimate truth of all conventional truths is their being void of inherent existence. Conventional truths, i.e. empirical phenomena, exist dependently upon causal conditions, parts and imputation; they have absolutely no existence apart from these conditioning factors. To assume that they do is to apprehend them as inherently existent. To understand that such inherent existence is and always has been utterly non-existent and merely a deep-rooted figment of the imagination is to understand the ultimate truth of conventional phenomena: i.e. their being void of inherent existence. In fact, conventional truths are only understood as they really are *after* we have understood their ultimate nature of voidness.

Throughout his explanations of the *Heart of Wisdom* and *Mahāmudrā*, Geshé Rabten closely follows Tsong Khapa's tradition of interpretation. In order to maintain consistency of presentation, the *Guide to the Middle Way* has also been translated in strict accordance with Tsong Khapa's own commentary to the text, his *Clear Illumination of the Intention*. Since this present work is not specifically intended for an academic audience, I have taken the liberty of not making any typographical or other distinctions between the words of Chandrakīrti's root text and the additional material from Tsong Khapa's commentary. In this way the reader is presented with a more legible text, unpunctuated by notations that may often distract one from the actual content.

Geshé Rabten was born in the mountainous and remote province of Kham in Eastern Tibet in 1920. His early years were spent as a farm boy, working in his father's fields and tending sheep in the surrounding hills. However, at the age of nineteen he met some monks from his home province who had just returned from several years of study in the monasteries of Lhasa. Inspired by their example of learning and tranquility, he decided to leave home and devote himself to the monastic life. Having obtained his father's permission, he set out on the long and arduous journey to Central Tibet.

Upon arriving in Lhasa he enrolled in the monastic university of Sera and thereupon began a course of study and contemplation that would engage him for the next twenty years until his departure for India. His studies consisted of an exhaustive inquiry into the various doctrines of Buddhism. Along with the other students he was trained in the art of dialectical analysis and proceeded to apply this technique to the subjects of logic, epistemology and metaphysics. The sessions of study were broken by periods during which the monks were encouraged to contemplate further the meaning of the teachings in the solitude of meditational retreat.

In 1959, however, he was forced to flee Tibet and seek refuge in India because the prevailing political situation under Chinese occupation made further stay in Lhasa impossible. While in India he was able to continue his training and within a few years completed the entire course of study and passed his final examinations. It was around this time that he was appointed a religious assistant to His Holiness the Dalai Lama. In this new role he received permission to withdraw from communal monastic life and for several years lived in retreat in a tiny hermitage in the hills behind Dharamsala.

In 1969 the Dalai Lama asked him to start giving instruction to the small but steadily growing number of Westerners interested in exploring the traditions of Tibetan Buddhism. A group of disciples formed around him and five years later he was invited to Switzerland to give a meditation course near Geneva. Following this he was appointed abbot of the Tibetan Monastic Institute in Rikon, near Zürich, where he began training several Western students in the same course of study that he himself had followed. To make this training more widely available he founded Tharpa Choeling, Centre for Higher Tibetan Studies, in Mont Pèlerin near Vevey, Switzerland, and in 1979 settled there as full-time spiritual director.

In all his teachings Geshé Rabten emphasizes that a fully integrated spiritual life requires a sound foundation and needs to be cultivated patiently and gradually. It is not a question of gaining some sudden illumination, clairvoyance or supernormal powers; these are mere moments within a much richer process and, in themselves, not of very great importance. The development of the mind must be seen in the context of a graduated path culminating in complete enlightenment. Only with such a broad outlook can a true sense of spiritual perspective be gained. It is important, therefore, to begin by taking stock of our present situation, recognizing our current state of being and becoming fully conscious of the diverse potentialities within us.

Certain potentialities lead to distorted and disturbed psychological states which, in turn, bring about disharmonious forms of behaviour. These destructive qualities preventing us from living a full and wholesome existence need to be eliminated from the mind in the same way that a cancerous growth needs to be removed from the body. Once again it must be stressed that there is no instant cure. Nor is it of any help simply to supress these tendencies. The process of resolving these inner conflicts permanently is a task that requires complete honesty with oneself, precise knowledge of the workings of one's mind and determination to undergo the often painful experience of self-transformation. However, in addition to many negative tendencies — such as desirous attachment, hatred and ignorance — we are also endowed with positive qualities which, when developed, perform the two-fold function of counteracting the negative potentialities and leading us progressively to a more intelligent and wholesome state of being. The graduated path (*lam.rim*) is a stage-by-stage description of this process of spiritual purification and development. Through adopting it as the framework for our practice we are able to avoid self-deception and gain instead a proper sense of direction. The end-result is achievment of the state of a buddha in which the inner purpose of one's own being is fully realized and the capacity for a truly authentic relationship with others is brought to its ultimate fulfilment.

Preparation is a word that frequently occurs in Geshé Rabten's discourses. He often uses the example of someone building a house. If the person has not gathered the necessary materials, prepared the ground and so forth, it would be absurd for him to consider building anything. Likewise, in spiritual development it is senseless to attempt the more advanced and "exotic" meditational practices unless one has first cultivated a firm psychological and moral basis for them. This requires living in accordance with sound ethical principles, purifying the gross disturbing elements of consciousness and developing strong wholesome tendencies.

Religious experience is not some alien quality that can be miraculously introduced into our present confused and distracted existence. It is achieved, on the contrary, through our *becoming* religious. A genuine spiritual life is not one consisting of a series of disconnected and undefined experiences occurring at random; it is a constant dynamic process incorporating every element of our being. As such it needs to proceed from a firm ground and, in turn, become the ground for its subsequent development. Nowadays, we are used to rapid changes and instant results, but by projecting these expectations onto our spiritual life we only hinder its progress. However inconvenient and time-consuming it may appear, we have to accept the harsh spiritual reality that the untangling of our deep-rooted psychological problems requires patient and systematic application of the necessary remedies.

One thing in particular that is noteworthy about Geshé Rabten's teachings is their scope and diversity. His talks often present themselves in the form of a fabric composed of numerous different threads; logical analysis is juxtaposed with devotional prayer while complex philosophical concepts are starkly illustrated by simple earthy images. There is no seemingly unbridgeable gulf between theory and practice. To think analytically ceases to be a mere intellectual exercise when, through such a teacher's example, it is seen to operate within the context of a spiritual discipline. It becomes, instead, an integral part of the growth of the whole person. Likewise, meditation is not reduced to the level of mere emotions and feelings where all intellectual operations are considered a hindrance. In short, for religion to be a vital elements of life it needs to take into account all the diverse elements of the person. Otherwise it becomes either a system of arid dogma or a collection of mere techniques and therapies.

For a detailed biographical study of Geshé Rabten as well as for a more elaborate introduction to his teachings, the reader is referred to the *Life and Teachings of Geshé Rabten*. In many respects this book is a development of several of the main themes originally presented there.

Finally, I would like to thank the Tibetisches Zentrum, Hamburg, for having provided me with the occasion to complete this work, and in particular Geshé Thubten Ngawang for his valuable explanations of the *Guide to the Middle Way*.

Stephen Batchelor
(Gelong Jhampa Thabkay)
Hamburg, 1980

Part One
The Heart of Wisdom

A Discourse on the Essence
of the Sacred Mother:
the Perfection of Wisdom

Contents of Part One

Preface to Part One

The *Heart of Wisdom* is one of the best-known and most popular of Mahāyāna Buddhist sutras. It treats in a summarized yet coherent manner the essential contents of the more extensive *Perfection of Wisdom Sutras*. Its form is that of a spontaneous dialogue between the bodhisattva Avalokiteshvara and the arhat Shāriputra inspired through the power of the Buddha's concentration. The sutra is especially renowned as one of the most radical presentations of the *via negativa* approach found in the history of religious thinking.

In his commentary to the text, Geshé Rabten first places this sutra in the general context of the Buddha's teachings and then proceeds to clarify its central theme of voidness. He pays special attention to the significance and the extent of application of the negative dialectic employed in the sutra to induce an understanding of voidness. In addition, he explains how the seemingly negative content of the discourse implicitly affirms its positive counterpart of a structured path to enlightenment.

The commentary was given as a public seminar at Tharpa Choeling, Centre for Higher Tibetan Studies, Switzerland, from the 23rd to the 26th of May 1980.

1 The Text of the Heart of Wisdom

Thus I have heard. At one time the Lord was sitting on Vulture's Peak near the city of Rajgir. He was accompanied by a large community of monks as well as a large community of bodhisattvas. On that occasion the Lord was absorbed in a particular concentration
5 called the profound appearance. Meanwhile the bodhisattva, the great being, the noble Avalokiteshvara was contemplating the profound discipline of the perfection of wisdom. He came to see that the five aggregates were void of any inherent nature of their own.

Through the power of the Buddha, the venerable Shāriputra
10 approached the noble Avalokiteshvara and asked him, "How should a son of the noble lineage proceed when he wants to train in the profound discipline of the perfection of wisdom?"

The noble Avalokiteshvara replied to the venerable Shāriputra, "Whatever son or daughter of the noble lineage wants to train in
15 the profound discipline of the perfection of wisdom should consider things in the following way. First, he or she should clearly and thoroughly comprehend that the five aggregates are void of any inherent nature of their own. Form is void, but voidness is form. Voidness is not other than forms and forms are
20 not other than voidness. Similarly, feelings, discernments, formative elements and consciousness are also void. Likewise, Shāriputra, are all phenomena void. They have no defining characteristics; they are unproduced; they do not cease; they are

undefiled, yet they are not separate from defilement; they do not decrease, yet they do not increase. This being the case, Shāriputra, in terms of voidness there exist no forms, no feelings, no discernments, no formative elements, no consciousness; no eyes, no ears, no noses, no tongues, no bodies, no minds; no visual-forms, no sounds, no smells, no tastes, no tactile sensations, no mental-objects. There exist no visual elements, no mental elements, and no elements of mental consciousness. There exist no ignorance and no exhaustion of ignorance, no ageing and death and no exhaustion of ageing and death. In the same way there exist no suffering, no origin of suffering, no cessation, no path, no wisdom, no attainment and no lack of attainment.

"Therefore, Shāriputra, since bodhisattvas have no attainment, they depend upon and dwell in the perfection of wisdom; their minds are unobstructed and unafraid. They transcend all error and finally reach the end-point: nirvana.

"All the buddhas of the past, present and future have depended, do and will depend upon the perfection of wisdom. Thereby they became, are becoming and will become unsurpassably, perfectly and completely awakened buddhas.

"Therefore, the mantra of the perfection of wisdom is a mantra of great knowledge; it is an unsurpassable mantra; it is a mantra that is comparable to the incomparable; it is a mantra that totally pacifies all suffering. It will not deceive you, therefore know it to be true! I proclaim the mantra of the perfection of wisdom: *tayathā gate gate pāragate pārasamgate bodhi svāhā*. Shāriputra, it is in this way that the great bodhisattvas train themselves in the profound perfection of wisdom."

At that moment the Lord arose from his concentration and said to the noble Avalokiteshvara, "Well said, well said. That is just how it is, my son, just how it is. The profound perfection of wisdom should be practised exactly as you have explained it. Then the tathāgatas will be truly delighted."

When the Lord had spoken these words, the venerable Shāriputra and the bodhisattva, the great being, the noble Avalokiteshvara, and the entire gathering of gods, humans, asuras and gandharvas were overjoyed, and they praised what the Lord had said.

2 The Commentary to the Heart of Wisdom

Introduction

The text that I am going to explain here is a sutra called the *Heart of Wisdom*. This short scripture was taught by the Buddha himself and contains the heart or the essence of what is discussed in the entire body of the *Perfection of Wisdom* literature. However, although the content of the sutra itself is very profound, making it fully meaningful depends upon the motivation with which we approach it. We should not study such teachings either with the motivation to gain thereby some temporal satisfaction during this present limited existence or with the intention merely to be able to derive some personal well-being for ourselves alone. Instead, we should try to understand what is being taught in order that we may be able subsequently to accomplish the welfare of all other living beings.

What is it that we are ultimately seeking? If we seriously ponder this question, we shall come to the conclusion that we are seeking to be totally free from all problems, all the negative aspects of our existence, and to realize fully all positive and wholesome qualities. Although such an intention may not always be conscious in our

minds, nevertheless, upon analysis we shall find that it is a fundamental motivating force behind everything we do. It goes without
saying that all of us would regard such a state of being, were it to
be attained, as highly desirable. In Buddhism such a state, in
which all negativities have been uprooted and all positive qualities
realized, is called buddhahood.

This state of being of a buddha is regarded as having two
principal aspects, namely, the *dharmakāya* (truth body) and the
rūpakāya (form body). These two bodies, however, cannot be
realized independently or sequentially but only simultaneously;
the attainment of one invariably necessitates the attainment of the
other. Nevertheless they are two resultant aspects of buddhahood,
and therefore, although they occur simultaneously, we can still
speak of them as having their own exclusive causes. The cause for
the dharmakāya is wisdom or the accumulation of wisdom, and
the cause for the rūpakāya is method or the accumulation of merit.
Generally speaking, both wisdom and method can be said to act as
causes for both the dharmakāya and the rūpakāya. But since
wisdom acts as the principal cause for the dharmakāya and
method as the principal cause for the rūpakāya, they have subsequently come to be regarded as their exclusive causes.

Furthermore, various forms of wisdom are considered to
pertain to the accumulation of wisdom and thereby to be causes
for the dharmakāya. But among all these states of wisdom, one
alone is of supreme importance: the wisdom that understands
voidness. However, it must be emphasized that for someone who
seeks to attain the state of buddhahood, both causes, method as
well as wisdom, need to be cultivated equally. Nevertheless, in
comparison with the practice of wisdom, it is relatively easy to
understand how to practise method. The development of wisdom,
and in particular the development of the wisdom that understands
voidness, is much more difficult to achieve.

Voidness is often said to be profound. This is because it is so
difficult to understand. For the same reason, the sutras in which
voidness is taught are called the profound sutras. The Buddha
taught his disciples the meaning of voidness in great detail. On
some occasions he delivered very extensive discourses on the

subject, at other times briefer, more concise explanations. Three of the central teachings on voidness are the great, middle-length and shorter *Perfection of Wisdom Sutras*. The great sutra is composed of one hundred thousand verses, the middle-length sutra of twenty-five thousand verses and the shorter sutra of eight thousand verses. In all of these sutras, however, a complete explanation of both aspects of the path to buddhahood, i.e. wisdom and method, is given. But since their principal subject matter is that of voidness they are said to expound explicitly the wisdom aspect of the path while only implicitly treating the method aspect.

In addition to these three sutras there are also many others that deal with the subject of voidness, but they are too numerous to list now. The sutra we will be studying here is called the *Heart of Wisdom*. It is so called because it is a discourse (sutra) that explains the very heart or essence of all the *Perfection of Wisdom Sutras*, and just as the longer *Perfection of Wisdom Sutras* teach both aspects of the path — wisdom explicitly and method implicitly — so too are they both dealt with in the *Heart of Wisdom*. How the *Heart of Wisdom* explains the practices of both wisdom and method will be clarified below.

Before embarking on the explanation of the sutra itself, it is necessary to point out exactly what is meant by the term "sutra." A sutra of the Buddha is equivalent to the words or the speech of the Buddha. However, three kinds of Buddha-words can be distinguished:

1. *Words spoken by the Buddha himself*: any advice or teaching that the Buddha personally delivered to his disciples. Examples would be the three *Perfection of Wisdom Sutras* mentioned above.

2. *Words spoken with the permission of the Buddha*: passages in the sutras that were not actually spoken by the Buddha himself. An example would be the introductory passages that explain where and when the sutra was given and so forth. Even though they were not spoken by the Buddha, these words are regarded as sutra because they accurately report the circumstances in which particular teachings were given. Many of Buddha's disciples achieved a state of concentration enabling them to remember

without mistake or distortion not only the word-for-word teachings of the Buddha but also where they were given and to whom. Later, after Buddha's passing, it became necessary for these gifted disciples to come together periodically and recite Buddha's discources so that they would not be forgotten in the future. These special occasions came to be known as the times when the Buddha's words were gathered together or compiled. One might suspect that such a system of recording the teachings would be open to much abuse, that some disciples would have forgotten exactly what was said or would take such opportunities to express their own ideas. But we should bear in mind that these disciples not only had tremendous powers of memory but fully understood the meaning and significance of what the Buddha had said. There was, therefore, really no danger of corruption.

3. *Words that originated from the Buddha's blessing*: these are of three kinds: words that arose from the blessing of the Buddha's body, speech and mind respectively. An example of a sutra that originated from the blessing of the Buddha's body would be the *Ten Grounds Sutra*. An example of a sutra that originated from the blessing of the Buddha's speech would be the *Relieving the Remorse of Ajātashatra Sutra*. Words that arose from the blessing of the Buddha's mind are also of three types: those that arose from the blessing of the power of truth, wisdom and the concentration present in his mind. What is meant by the power of truth in the Buddha's mind is a particular intention or wish he possesses that is able to influence the experiences of others. For example, when wind blows through the leaves of a tree usually we hear nothing but a rustling sound; but when such a phenomenon has been blessed by the power of truth in the Buddha's mind, it may be experienced as a teaching of dharma. Teachings communicated in such a way would be examples of words that originated from the blessing of the power of truth in the Buddha's mind.

On other occasions teachings occur through the force of the blessing of Buddha's wisdom. These can be spoken by someone who has no acquaintance with or knowledge of dharma at all, but who nevertheless spontaneously and unintentionally utters words that communicate the meaning of dharma. This happens because of that person's being blessed in that moment by the wisdom of the Buddha's mind. It might seem strange that the rustling of leaves or the unintentional utterances of someone are considered as words or sutras of Buddha. However, although they are not directly spoken by the Buddha himself, since they are words that come about from his blessings, they are technically considered as sutras.

An example of a sutra that arose from the blessing of the Buddha's concentration is the *Heart of Wisdom*, the text I am going to explain here. The reason why the two previous categories of Buddha's speech were presented in such detail was to enable us to understand exactly where to place *The Heart of Wisdom* in the general context of the Buddha's teachings. The precise reason why it is said to have originated from the blessing of the Buddha's concentration will be explained as we go through the sutra itself.

The introductory passages of the sutra

The Tibetan text starts by giving the title of the sutra, first in transliterated Sanskrit, *Bhagavatiprajñāpāramitāhṛdya*, and then in Tibetan, which, when translated, means: the *Essence of the Sacred Mother: the Perfection of Wisdom*.

The perfection of wisdom refers specifically to the wisdom that directly and intuitively understands the voidness of all phenomena. This wisdom is said to be the sacred mother because it is the mother of, i.e. that which gives rise to, the sacred ones, namely the buddhas. It is through developing an understanding of voidness in one's own mind that one is enabled finally to realize the state of buddhahood. Just as a child cannot be born without a mother, likewise a buddha cannot be born without relying upon the "mother" of the perfection of wisdom. However, this is just one reason why the perfection of wisdom is referred to as the mother (or, more strictly speaking, why it is put in the feminine gender). Another reason is to indicate that the perfection of wisdom pertains to the wisdom aspect of the path (which is traditionally associated with the female) as opposed to the method aspect of the path (traditionally associated with the male).

The sutra itself starts with an introductory passage that mentions who gave the teaching, where it was given, to whom and so forth. These first lines of the text belong to the second category of Buddha's words, i.e. words spoken with the permission of the Buddha. These words are in fact those of the arhat who recollected and compiled this sutra after the Buddha's decease, but it is not exactly clear which disciple of the Buddha was responsible for this. There were no doubt many arhats present at the teaching, but I would think it most likely that Ānanda is the one who is heard introducing this sutra. He begins,

(1) Thus I have heard. At one time . . .

The time at which the sutra was given is not precisely recorded in terms of years and months; the text simply states, "At one time . . . ." However, these words indicate two important points: the great power of memory and understanding of the compiler to be able to recall what was said on that one occasion and the rarity of such a teaching, which was given only *one* time. The compiler continues,

> . . . the Lord was sitting on Vulture's Peak near the city of Rajgir.

Here the teacher of the sutra and the place of teaching are mentioned. The teacher is the Lord, an epithet referring to the Buddha. The place is Vulture's Peak, a small mountain just outside the city of Rajgir, in present-day Bihar, India.

The next line describes the beings to whom the discourse was delivered,

> He was accompanied by a large community of monks as well as a large community of bodhisattvas.

Although the only members of the audience specifically mentioned in the text are the communities of monks and bodhisattvas, it should be understood that a far wider variety of beings were in fact present. From this world there would have been shrāvakas, pratyekabuddhas and many men and women who had taken the Buddhist lay precepts. Numerous beings from worlds other than our own also would have been present.

This world in which we live is not the only inhabited region in the universe. In addition, there are countless other world systems containing various types of beings. Some of these worlds are impure, whereas others are pure realms in which the inhabitants live beyond the cycle of compulsive birth and death. Before Buddha gave a particular discourse many rays of light would miraculously radiate from his heart and shine out to the furthest reaches of the universe. They would strike all these realms and cause them to vibrate in a certain way. These vibrations would indicate to those inhabitants who were capable of perceiving them that in India, in our world, the Buddha Shākyamuni was about to give a discourse on a particular subject, in this case, the perfection of wisdom. Many of these beings would then spontaneously appear hovering in space around where the Buddha was preparing to speak. We may think that the Buddha would be inaudible to such a large audience. However, one of the special qualities of a buddha's speech is that it can be heard with exactly the same degree of clarity whether one is sitting close by him or very far away.

> On that occasion the Lord was absorbed in a particular concentration called the profound appearance.

After the description of those who were assembled, attention is now turned to the Buddha himself. As the *Heart of Wisdom* was about to be delivered we find him absorbed in meditation upon what is called the profound appearance. In general "profound appearance" refers simply to voidness. In other words, the Buddha was dwelling in single-pointed concentration upon voidness, i.e. the true nature of all phenomena. More specifically, however, profound appearance has a two-fold connotation: it indicates the two truths — ultimate and conventional — and the relation between them. "Profound" refers to the ultimate truth of voidness, which, as we shall see later, is defined as the mere absence of inherent existence. "Appearance" refers to the conventional truths that appear to us and perform functions although their ultimate nature is one of voidness of any inherent existence. These two truths should also be understood in relation to wisdom and method, the two aspects of the path to buddhahood. Wisdom is developed primarily through gaining insight into ultimate truth, whereas method is cultivated in the context of conventional truths.

Throughout the delivery of the *Heart of Wisdom* the Buddha remains in this state of silent concentration and only at the conclusion of the discourse does he actually say anything. Nevertheless, the sutra is attributed to him, not because he actually spoke it, but because he caused it to take place through the power of his concentration. Thus these words of the Buddha belong to the third category of the Buddha's words and, specifically, originated from the blessing of the Buddha's concentration.

Two of the principal members of the audience at this time were the arhat Shāriputra and the bodhisattva Avalokiteshvara. Shāriputra is commonly regarded as a shrāvaka arhat and the most learned and wise of the Buddha's disciples. Avalokiteshvara is usually presented as a bodhisattva renowned for his compassion. In fact it is difficult to say exactly what level of realization these two disciples had achieved. It is frequently acknowledged that Avalokiteshvara, for example, was in fact a fully awakened buddha.

Through the power of the Buddha's concentration these two disciples became involved in a dialogue. This took place quite spontaneously and without any intention on their behalf. The content of their entire conversation was determined solely by the power of the Buddha's concentration. Furthermore, because they themselves had already achieved a complete understanding of voidness, they were not speaking for their own benefit. The purpose of their dialogue was to clarify the meaning of voidness to those disciples who did not yet understand it and to improve the understanding of those who had only partially understood it.

The text now goes on to describe how the dialogue came about.

(5) Meanwhile the bodhisattva, the great being, the noble Avalokiteshvara was contemplating the profound discipline of the perfection of wisdom. He came to see that the five aggregates were void of any inherent nature of their own.

As well as the Buddha, the bodhisattva Avalokiteshvara was also absorbed in single-pointed concentration upon voidness. But then, through the power of the Buddha's concentration, he was caused to arise from his state of deep contemplation, in which he beheld nothing but voidness, and to become conscious once more of conventional phenomena. At this moment he recognized that the five aggregates, i.e. all conditioned phenomena, are able to appear and function even though their ultimate nature is one of being void of any inherent existence. It was only through interrupting his concentration that he was now able to engage in a dialogue with Shāriputra. No verbal communication would have been possible had he remained in a state of deep absorption.

> Through the power of the Buddha, the venerable
(10) Shāriputra approached the noble Avalokiteshvara and asked him, "How should a son of the noble lineage proceed when he wants to train in the profound discipline of the perfection of wisdom?"

Likewise, the power of the Buddha's concentration blessed Shāriputra, inspiring him to approach Avalokiteshvara and ask him about the means of developing an understanding of voidness. He phrases his question in terms of a "son of the noble lineage who wants to train. . . ." "A son of the noble lineage" refers to anyone, man or woman, who aspires to an understanding of voidness. Since such an aspiration brings a person closer to the state of buddhahood, he is thereby regarded as entering the lineage of the Buddha. This means that he tends towards the type or the character of a buddha. Shāriputra also addresses his question on behalf of those who *want* to train in the discipline of the perfection of wisdom. This implies that teachings on voidness can be of any real meaning only to those who have a definite interest in understanding them. It would be quite fruitless to give such teachings to people who are not so inclined.

Avalokiteshvara's presentation of the perfection of wisdom

The noble Avalokiteshvara replied to the venerable

Shāriputra, "Whatever son or daughter of the noble
(15) lineage wants to train in the profound discipline of the
perfection of wisdom shoud consider things in the
following way."

The reply that Avalokiteshvara now proceeds to give Shāriputra
constitutes the main body of the rest of the sutra. Once again we
should bear in mind that the attention of the audience is focused
not upon the Buddha, who is perhaps sitting to one side in meditation, but upon the dialogue taking place between the two disciples
Avalokiteshvara and Shāriputra. Avalokiteshvara starts to set
forth the way in which any son or daughter of the noble lineage
should meditate on voidness. It should be noted that he says
"*Whatever* son or daughter . . . ." This emphasizes the fact that the
perfection of wisdom is something that can be attained by all
people, whether they are men or women, rich or poor, monks or
laymen.

We often think of buddhahood, or enlightenment, as something
very far away from us and practically unattainable. But we should
remember that enlightenment is a result that arises in dependence
upon its own particular causes. If we possess the cause, the result
will inevitably occur. This means that if we earnestly study,
contemplate and meditate, the result of buddhahood will definitely come about. But if we fail to make sufficient effort, then
no matter how much we may wish for enlightenment, it will never
come.

Before continuing with the text itself, it is necessary to clarify
what is meant by the term "voidness." Much of the following discussion will be quite meaningless if we do not know exactly what
voidness is: we shall fail to understand the text and may easily
develop a confused and misleading conception of what is being
taught. Although it is not easy to grasp the significance of
voidness, it is most important to consider carefully what it means
and not jump to any premature conclusions.

The first misconception about voidness to be overcome is that it
is something precious and holy. Often people consider voidness to
be an object of devotion and worship, similar to the Buddha.

Voidness is neither holy nor precious; it has no particular value in itself. However, the *understanding* of voidness is something very precious, meaningful and holy. This understanding is equivalent to the perfection of wisdom: a state of consciousness that is worthy of much devotion and respect.

Furthermore, voidness is not something that exists separately, in a realm of its own, apart from the phenomena of the empirical world. It is a quality present in every existent phenomenon, without exception. As soon as an entity comes into existence, so does its voidness; the very moment that an entity ceases to exist, its voidness also disappears. Voidness is an essential quality of everything that exists. All phenomena have two distinct modes of being: the ultimate and conventional. Voidness is the ultimate mode of being of every phenomenon; it is the way in which phenomena actually exist.

No single phenomenon lacks the quality of being a dependently arising event. Thus every phenomenon is said to be a "dependent arising." Nevertheless, all things instinctively appear to us as though they did exist independently, as though they were endowed with their own autonomous self-existence. Take for example a mountain. From its own side, it seems to have an inherent substantiality and massiveness independent of all conditions. It stands there against us: imposing, independent and concrete. But upon reflection we shall slowly become aware that this mountain depends for its existence upon a variety of causes and conditions as well as innumerable atomic particles that are so small we cannot see them. It is only through the assembly of all these different particles, each one depending on the others, that the mountain comes into being. Only in this *dependent* manner does the mountain exist; there is no independently existent entity "mountain" somehow subsisting apart from the causes and component parts that constitute the basis for its being.

The same is true for all material phenomena, however large or small they may be. Imagine that one is holding a grape in one's hand. If one considers just this small, relatively insignificant object, one will start to notice the vast number of diverse conditions that were responsible for its present existence. Just think of the field in which it was grown, the vine from which it came, the efforts of the farmer, the sun and the rain that helped it grow. In this way we can understand how every phenomenon is dependent for its existence upon a whole multitude of conditioning factors. There is nothing to be found that lacks such a dependent existence. Even the tiny atomic particles that are the basic constituents of matter are dependent events. They depend upon their directional parts, as well as the causes that produced them and the effects that they in turn produce.

Likewise, less concrete phenomena, such as time, are also dependently arising. Take for example this year 1980. It appears to us as though it were a solid chunk of time bearing its own fixed identity. However, it only comes into being in dependence upon shorter periods of time: months, weeks and days, which in turn are dependent upon hours, minutes, seconds, milliseconds and so forth. There is no year or other period of time that exists independently of shorter periods of time. If one were to remove any one of the component moments, the whole would be unable to exist.

The mind too has no independent existence. Any one state of mind depends upon numerous moments of consciousness and various mental factors. A mind that has been meditating for an hour appears to have an independent self-identity. But upon analysis it is found to be utterly dependent upon the various individual thoughts, perceptions and feelings that occurred during the hour, as well as upon the objects the mind was contemplating. The individual mental factors — for example, feelings of pleasure and pain — are also dependent upon a variety of conditions that, once assembled, cause a particular feeling to occur. The beginningless and endless stream of consciousness that passes from one life to another and finally reaches buddhahood is not independently existent either. It is in a constant state of momentary change and thus depends upon the infinite number of moments that constitute its continuity.

The person is also dependent. We can talk of a person as *having* a body and a mind, but we cannot identify the person with either body or mind. We cannot think of someone as being his bones or his flesh, nor can we consider him to be one of his states of perception or consciousness. In reality, the person exists merely in dependence upon the physical and mental components of which he is constituted. Thus he has no inherent independent existence apart from these things, but neither is he identical with them.

Even permanent, unconditioned phenomena such as abstract-space are dependent entities. The abstract-space, i.e. the mere lack of obstructive contact, in this room is dependent upon its directional parts, i.e. the lack of obstructive contact in the different parts of the room.

In addition to being dependent upon causes and parts, phenomena are also dependent upon their being imputed by the mind. This is a much subtler mode of dependence and is more difficult to understand than dependence on causes and parts. However, it is very important to grasp what this means. It is often said that all phenomena are merely imputed by the mind and that nothing whatsoever can exist independently of such imputation. But what does it mean to impute something with the mind? Actually, to impute (*btags.pa*) means nothing more than to apprehend (*'dzin.pa*). We may think of a lamp in our room at home. In thinking of it we apprehend it, and in apprehending it we are "imputing" it. Thus imputation is the mind's fundamental quality of apprehending objects.

We can apprehend, or impute, both existent and non-existent entities. If what we apprehend is existent, the mind that apprehends it is a valid mind, whereas if we apprehend something that does not exist, the mind that apprehends it is mistaken. For example, we may walk into the garden and notice a longish, slightly coiled object partially concealed in the high grass. We immediately recognize it as a snake and stand back in fear. However, as we cautiously approach the snake for a closer look, we suddenly realize that it is not a snake at all, but the garden hose. Thus the initial perception imputed a snake, but since its object was not in reality a snake, the perception was mistaken. Nevertheless, on other occasions we may see an object and correctly apprehend it as a snake. In this case the imputation of a snake is in accordance with reality and the mind that apprehends a snake is thereby a valid mind. Therefore, when it is said that all existent phenomena are imputations of the mind, we must understand that "mind" in this sense means a *valid* mind. It does not mean that an existent phenomenon is something that can just be imagined by any particular state of mind.

All phenomena exist in dependence upon causes and conditions (if they are conditioned phenomena), component parts and mental imputation. This being the case we can conclude that nothing has any autonomous existence independent of causes, parts and imputation. Whatever appears to us as existing inherently and not dependently is called "that which is negated in voidness." Now, that which is negated here, i.e. inherent, independent existence, is utterly non-existent; but the voidness of it is existent. *Voidness is the mere absence of what is negated.* If what was to be negated — inherent existence — were existent, voidness would then be non-existent. However, as soon as something comes into existence, it is, in its very nature, something merely imputed by the mind and thereby void of any independent existence. Therefore, what we mean by voidness is the sheer lack or absence of any inherent, independent existence within phenomena.

Consider for example a rosary. A rosary is dependent upon its being imputed by the mind. Therefore, it does not exist as an autonomous entity independent of mental imputation. The rosary's mere lack of independent, autonomous existence is the voidness of the rosary. And this voidness is the ultimate mode of being of the rosary. On the other hand, the rosary that is merely an imputation of the mind is the conventionally existent rosary. Thus there are two aspects to the rosary: its ultimate mode of being and its conventional mode of being. But although we think of these two aspects as distinct qualities, in essence they are identical. That is to say, the rosary's being merely a mental imputation and its being void of existing independently of mental imputation can be thought of and spoken of as distinct, but in reality they are one thing.

By positing the existence of phenomena in this twofold way we avoid falling into the two extreme positions of permanence and annihilation. Through denying that all phenomena have any inherent, independent existence, we avoid the extreme view of permanence (which regards things as inherently existent). But in affirming that all phenomena do exist imputedly and dependently, we escape also the extreme view of annihilation (which denies that phenomena exist at all). In their very nature phenomena are free from these two extremes, since they do not inherently exist yet do imputedly exist. Therefore, they are said to abide naturally in the middle way (*mādhyamaka*).

I shall now continue to explain the text of the *Heart of Wisdom*. Throughout it is very important to bear in mind what has been said above concerning the nature of voidness. This sutra contains many negative expressions: "there are no forms, no feelings, no minds" and so forth. However, we should always remember exactly what is negated when speaking of voidness. It is not phenomena themselves that are being negated but inherently existent phenomena that seem to be independent of mental imputation.

In the text so far Avalokiteshvara has just started giving his reply to Shāriputra's question. He continues,

> "First, he or she should clearly and thoroughly comprehend that the five aggregates are void of any inherent nature of their own."

Avalokiteshvara begins by emphasizing that anyone who wants to develop the perfection of wisdom must understand that none of the five aggregates exists inherently, independently of mental imputation. The five aggregates are one way of classifying all conditioned phenomena. They are (1) the aggregate of forms, (2) the aggregate of feelings, (3) the aggregate of discernments, (4) the aggregate of formative elements and (5) the aggregate of consciousness.

> "Form is void, but voidness is form. Voidness is not (20) other than forms and forms are not other than voidness."

Avalokiteshvara begins by considering the aggregate of forms. He points out that forms, such as the material elements of the body for example, are void of any inherent, autonomous existence. But he immediately goes on to affirm the essential identity of form with its voidness of inherent existence. He states that voidness is form, meaning that the voidness of the inherent existence of form is essentially identical with form. The same point is made even clearer in the following sentence. There he asserts that the voidness of form is not essentially distinct from form and neither is form essentially distinct from its voidness. The two modes of being of form — its ultimate truth of being void of inherent existence and its conventional truth of being merely a mental imputation — are shown in these lines to be essentially identical although conceptually distinct. For someone who has gained genuine insight into this point, when perceiving form he likewise understands it to be void of inherent existence, and when he contemplates the voidness of form he is fully aware of the fact that conventionally form validly appears and functions.

Such insight into form automatically counteracts the disturbing conceptions such as attachment and aversion that we habitually have with regard to form. This happens because such an understanding is the direct opponent to the ignorant grasping at the inherent existence of form which acts as the basis for all other disturbing conceptions of it. Of the five aggregates, form is mentioned first because it is that which usually gives rise to the greatest amount of attachment and other disturbing conceptions. Once we have understood the nature of form as described here, the following explanation of the remaining aggregates will be relatively straightforward.

> "Similarly, feelings, discernments, formative elements and consciousness are also void."

Feelings too are void of any inherent existence, yet that voidness of inherent existence is essentially identical with the feelings. Thus exactly the same considerations we made with regard to forms should also be applied here to feelings.

The aggregate of feeling is composed primarily of the experiences of pleasure and pain. These are mental factors. When we have a pain in the knee, the pain is not identifiable with the bones and muscles, but is a mental experience that arises upon the basis of a particular configuration of physical elements. These feelings of pleasure and pain play a very great role in our lives. When we say that all beings in samsara are basically striving to find happiness and avoid suffering, this means that they are seeking the *feeling* of happiness and trying to dispel the *feeling* of suffering. However, the fulfilment of this goal forever seems to elude them. Happiness always declines into sorrow and the absence of suffering is invariably replaced by some conflict or frustration. But by contemplating that these feelings are void of any inherent existence, we can resolve these feeling-associated problems.

Discernment is the mind's quality of distinguishing and identifying its objects. It is possible to discern things in both a positive and a negative way. If we discern something in a positive, realistic manner, we find all ensuing communication with others to be fruitful and free from conflict. But if our discernment is negative and unrealistic, there is a great danger that problems such as one-sidedness and fanaticism will follow, serving only to create disharmony. In order to counteract these negative discernments it is very helpful to meditate upon their voidness of inherent existence.

The aggregate of formative elements is composed of numerous wholesome and unwholesome mental factors. On the one hand it includes faith, compassion and wisdom; on the other, attachment, hatred and confusion. Considering the voidness of the unwholesome factors is a powerful means for overcoming them. The problem associated with the fifth aggregate, consciousness, is to regard it as a permanent essence of the person and equate it with the self. Reflection on the voidness of inherent existence of consciousness serves to dispel such misconceptions.

It was mentioned above that both the wisdom and method aspects of the path to buddhahood are taught in the *Heart of Wisdom*. Explicitly this sutra explains only the wisdom aspect, but implicitly the method aspect is also revealed. In fact all the stages of the path are tacitly propounded in the discourse. Specifically this is achieved through correlating the central passages of the text to the five paths: (1) the path of accumulation, (2) the path of preparation, (3) the path of seeing, (4) the path of meditation and (5) the path of no-more-learning. They correspond to the five principal stages on the path to enlightenment. Moreover, since these five paths correspond to the development of such practices as the thirty-seven facets of enlightenment and the ten powers of a buddha, the aspect of method is thereby implicitly shown. The path of accumulation corresponds to the four close placements of mindfulness, the four abandonments and the four miracle supports; the path of preparation to the five powers and the five strengths; the path of seeing to the seven limbs of enlightenment; the path of meditation to the eightfold noble path, and the path of no-more-learning to the ten powers of a buddha. These various divisions and correlations are explained in detail in the commentaries to the *Ornament of Clear Realization* of Maitreya.

The parts of Avalokiteshvara's answer to Shāriputra that we have explained so far (16-21) implicitly refer to the understanding of voidness of a person on the paths of accumulation and preparation. These first two of the five paths are those of ordinary beings, i.e. those who have not yet achieved the status of an ārya, that is, a noble being. But even though they are not āryas, they still have a valid understanding of voidness. The difference in understanding lies in the nature of their cognition of voidness. An ārya has a valid intuitive perception of voidness, whereas an ordinary being on the paths of accumulation and preparation has a valid inferential understanding which arises in dependence upon reasoning.

There are many stages in the understanding of voidness. At the very beginning we have to develop a sincere interest in the subject of voidness, listen to explanations of it, study and think about it. Gradually an idea of what voidness is will start to take clearer and clearer shape in our minds. But strictly speaking, this initial notion of voidness is not an understanding of voidness. In order to achieve a genuine understanding we need to analyze the nature of voidness with much reasoning. Through this process a conceptual understanding will eventually arise on the basis of a valid proof being established in our minds. This is the valid inferential understanding that occurs for those on the paths of accumulation and preparation. It is a firm state of knowledge and certainty, but because it still confuses voidness with one's mental image of voidness, it is not of the same quality as the ārya's intuitive understanding.

To reach such a level of insight it is necessary to develop single-pointed concentration upon the object of voidness that has been previously ascertained through analysis. Through constant and repeated acquaintance with voidness in this way, one reaches a point where the conceptual content fades away and one's vision of voidness becomes so immediate and clear that it seems as though there is no distinction between the voidness and the mind that is concentrating on it. The degree of immediacy and absorption attained at this point is compared to water being mixed with water. Just as one cannot separate water from two different sources once it has been poured into one container, so, at this point, is it impossible to separate the mind meditating on voidness from the voidness itself. When such an insight is reached one attains the path of seeing and becomes an ārya.

The text now continues by describing the characteristics of such an intuitive meditation on voidness.

> "Likewise, Shāriputra, are all phenomena void. They
> have no defining characteristics; they are unproduced;
> they do not cease; they are undefiled, yet they are not
> (25) separate from defilement; they do not decrease, yet they
> do not increase."

Once one has reached the path of seeing one realizes, non-conceptually and immediately, that every single phenomenon is void of any independent self-existence. The nature of this insight is further clarified in the text by listing certain qualities of the voidness perceived. It is said that phenomena are seen to be without defining characteristics. This, as well as the following qualifications, should not be taken literally. Generally speaking, phenomena *do* have defining characteristics; matter is defined as that which is composed of atoms and consciousness as that which is clear and knowing. What is meant here is that phenomena have no inherently existent defining characteristics that exhibit themselves independently of mental imputation. Likewise, phenomena are in fact produced from causes and they cease when the conditions for their existence no longer obtain. To say that phenomena are unproduced and do not cease means that they are not inherently produced and do not inherently cease independent of any other conditions.

Defilements, such as hatred, attachment and ignorance, also exist. But phenomena are said to be undefiled in the sense that they are not inherently defiled by such attitudes. To meditate on the non-inherent existence of the defilements is an effective way to overcome their domination over us. Likewise, when we attain enlightenment we become separated from defilements. But this state of being separated from defilement is not an inherently existent state. It only comes about in dependence upon actualizing the path and thus accumulating the necessary conditions that make it possible. Similarly our practice of dharma is subject to decrease and increase. Sometimes it seems to deteriorate and become weaker; at other times it grows and becomes stronger. But there is never any inherent decrease or increase that takes place independently of causes and conditions or mental imputation. It is in such ways that an ārya intuitively perceives all phenomena.

> "This being the case, Shāriputra, in terms of voidness there exist no forms, no feelings, no discernments, no formative elements, no consciousness; no eyes, no ears, no noses, no tongues, no bodies, no minds; no visual-forms, no sounds, no smells, no tastes, no tactile sensations, no
> (30) mental-objects. There exist no visual elements, no mental elements, and no elements of mental consciousness. There exist no ignorance and no exhaustion of ignorance, no ageing and death and no exhaustion of ageing and death. In the same way there exist no suffering, no origin
> (35) of suffering, no cessation, no path, no wisdom, no attainment and no lack of attainment."

In this long passage the meditation on voidness of an ārya on the path of meditation is described. The path of meditation follows the path of seeing and involves a longer and deeper acquaintance with the voidness than was perceived directly for the first time during the path of seeing. It is a process of continued and repeated absorption in the intuitive vision of voidness. Through the force of the path of meditation the instinctive disturbing conceptions are gradually uprooted, bringing one ever closer to the path of no-more-learning.

To emphasize that the path of meditation is a process of further acquaintance with what has been seen, the passage repeats that when meditating on voidness one · should recognize the five aggregates of form, feeling and so forth as having no inherent existence. And to indicate the extensiveness and greater profundity of this stage of meditation, further classifications of phenomena are also listed. First it is said that one should contemplate that the six sense bases — the eyes, ears and so forth — are void of any inherent self-existence. Likewise, the corresponding six objects of the six senses — visual-forms, sounds and so forth — should also be seen repeatedly as void. Next (30-31) the eighteen elements are listed in an abbreviated form. This eighteen-fold division into elements (*dhātu*) is simply a more elaborate way of classifying the twelve sense-fields (*āyatana*) mentioned previously (27-30).

Finally (31-35) there follows a contemplation of the non-inherent existence of the states of samsara and liberation and of the path to enlightenment. Samsara is described here in terms of the twelve links of dependent arising. The text mentions only the first link, ignorance, and the twelfth, ageing and death. These twelve links explain the dependent way in which the condition of cyclic existence comes about. An ārya on the path of meditation reflects upon how each of these twelve links is void of any inherent existence. Liberation, or nirvana, is referred to here as the exhaustion, i.e. the cessation, of the process of the twelve links of dependent arising. This state too should be understood to lack any inherent existence. Likewise, the four noble truths — suffering, the origin of suffering, cessation and the path — should also be seen to be void of independent, autonomous existence. Even the wisdom of the Buddha must be realized to be in its very nature void. Similarly all the attainments that one may gain along the path, as well as the state of having no attainments prior to engaging in the path, are also without any inherent existence. When reading or reciting this passage one must be clear that Avalokiteshvara does not intend to deny that all these things exist. Conventionally they do exist in dependence upon mental imputation and other conditions. All that is being denied is that they exist inherently and independently of such conditions.

> "Therefore, Shāriputra, since bodhisattvas have no attainment, they depend upon and dwell in the perfection of wisdom;"

This passage refers to the meditation on voidness of the bodhisattva who has reached what is called the end of the continuum. The end of the continuum is the very last moment on the path before one becomes a buddha. It is the final moment of existence as a sentient being. This moment is characterized by one's entering into a vajra-like, or adamantine, concentration on voidness that has the power finally to remove all the remaining obstacles to buddhahood. However, this state is still included in the path of meditation; only in the following moment is the fifth path of no-more-learning, i.e. buddhahood, realized.

> "their minds are unobstructed and unafraid. They transcend all error and finally reach the end-point: nirvana."

Here the state of buddhahood itself is described. As mentioned above, buddhahood is composed of two principal aspects: dharmakāya and rūpakāya. However, the dharmakāya is also further divided into the nature-dharmakāya and the wisdom-dharmakāya. The nature-dharmakāya refers to the final state of non-abiding nirvana realized in a buddha's mind. This is indicated in the text by the line: "their minds are unobstructed and unafraid." The wisdom-dharmakāya is the knowledge and insight of a buddha. This is referred to by the words: "They transcend all error." The rūpakāya, i.e. the aspect of a buddha that is accessible to others, is of two kinds: the saṃbhogakāya (the enjoyment body) and the nirmāṇakāya (emanation body). These two bodies become manifest for the sake of all sentient beings as soon as buddhahood is attained. As soon as all negative qualities are eliminated and all positive qualities are realized, the spontaneous activity of a buddha is able to manifest for the sake of others in the saṃbhogakāya and nirmāṇakāya forms. This rūpakāya aspect is specifically indicated by the words: "and finally reach the end-point: nirvana."

(40) "All the buddhas of the past, present and future have depended, do and will depend upon the perfection of wisdom. Thereby they became, are becoming and will become unsurpassably, perfectly and completely awakened buddhas."

This passage is a summary of all that has been said so far. It emphasizes the extreme importance and power of meditation upon voidness; for it is only through gaining and developing this insight that buddhahood is possible. All the beings in the past who have attained buddhahood, all those who are presently attaining it, and all those in the future who will attain it, must invariably depend upon an understanding of the voidness of inherent existence of all phenomena.

Therefore, the mantra of the perfection of wisdom is a (45) mantra of great knowledge; it is an unsurpassable mantra; it is a mantra that is comparable to the incomparable; it is a mantra that totally pacifies all suffering. It will not deceive you; therefore know it to be true!"

Because the understanding of voidness is so powerful it is compared to a mantra. Moreover, it is called the mantra of the perfection of wisdom because it has the ability to remove every single internal and external obstruction; it is called the mantra of great knowledge because through it we are able to overcome all distorted perceptions of external reality; it is called the unsurpassable mantra because it can destroy not only the distorted perceptions of external reality, but the distorted perceptions of every aspect of reality, both inner and outer. Buddhahood is often said to be incomparable. The understanding of voidness is called the mantra that is comparable to the incomparable because it is able actually to bring one to the level of buddhahood. Since it is capable of uprooting all the causes and conditions of suffering, it is given the name the mantra that totally pacifies all suffering. And because it is a practice that will never lead to any further confusion or deception, it should be understood as an infallible and true path to enlightenment.

Generally, the perfection of wisdom can be said to have two principal functions: supramundane and mundane. The supramundane function of the perfection of wisdom is that of taking us beyond the mundane condition of samsara — the domination of disturbing conceptions — to the transcendent state of buddhahood; by meditating on voidness we can gradually reach this goal. The mundane, or ordinary, function is that of acting as a means of overcoming temporary problems and difficulties like sickness, external interferences and so forth; by reciting texts such as the *Heart of Wisdom*, in which the perfection of wisdom is explained, we can overcome such obstacles.

Often the *Heart of Wisdom* is recited before dharma instructions are given, in order to dispel any obstacles to the understanding of the teaching. This is not just a Tibetan tradition but a practice originated by the Buddha himself. Usually, before delivering a discourse on the perfection of wisdom, he would request the deity Indra to recite the *Heart of Wisdom* in order to clear away any obstructing forces that would hinder the audience's understanding. In general it is very helpful to recite this sutra before engaging in any study or other dharma practice.

Thus the purpose of meditating on voidness and reciting the perfection of wisdom texts is to enable us to develop further along the path to enlightenment. But how, specifically, is this to be done? The answer is given in condensed form in the following line of the text:

"I proclaim the mantra of the perfection of wisdom: *tayathā gate gate pāragate pārasamgate bodhi svāhā.*"

Tayathā means "it is like this," in other words, "one should develop the perfection of wisdom in the following way." The first *gate* is interpreted here as meaning that one should firmly apply oneself to the practices of the path of accumulation. The next three words — *gate, pāragate* and *pārasamgate* — have the same meaning with respect to the paths of preparation, seeing and meditation respectively. Finally, *bodhi svāhā* means that one should strive to realize the fifth path, the path of no-more-learning: the state of buddhahood itself. Therefore, the perfection of wisdom is developed by means of progressively cultivating the five paths that culminate in buddhahood.

(50) "Shāriputra, it is in this way that the great bodhisattvas train themselves in the profound perfection of wisdom."

At the end of his explanation of the practice of the perfection of wisdom, Avalokiteshvara addresses Shāriputra once again by name and concludes that in such a way should a bodhisattva cultivate an understanding of voidness.

The Buddha's concluding remarks

At that moment the Lord arose from his concentration and said to the noble Avalokiteshvara, "Well said, well said. That is just how it is, my son, just how it is. The (55) profound perfection of wisdom should be practised exactly as you have explained it. Then the tathāgatas will be truly delighted."

Throughout the entire time Avalokiteshvara has been speaking the Buddha has remained silently absorbed in his meditation, inspiring the dialogue through the force of his concentration alone. But as soon as Avalokiteshvara finishes his explanation of the *Heart of Wisdom*, the Buddha comes out of his concentration and warmly congratulates him for what he has said. Twice he says, "Well said." The first time expresses his approval of the way in which Avalokiteshvara has clarified the causal aspects of the path. The second time shows an appreciation of Avalokiteshvara's treatment of the resultant state of buddhahood. To indicate how pleased he is with the discourse, he addresses Avalokiteshvara as "my son," a term that expresses much fondness and love. Finally, he confirms what has been taught by stating himself that the perfection of wisdom should indeed be practised as Avalokiteshvara has just explained. If someone should develop an understanding of voidness in such a way, he adds, all the buddhas will be pleased.

In conclusion the text describes the unanimous reaction of the various disciples to what the Buddha has just said:

> When the Lord had spoken these words, the venerable Shāriputra and the bodhisattva, the great being, the noble Avalokiteshavra, and the entire gathering of gods, (60) humans, asuras and gandharvas were overjoyed, and they praised what the Lord had said.

Part Two
A Guide to the Middle Way

A Translation
of the Sixth Chapter
of Chandrakīrti's
Mādhyamakāvatāra

Contents of Part Two

Preface to Part Two

This *Guide to the Middle Way* was composed by the Indian scholar Chandrakīrti during the sixth century A.D. It is designed as a commentary to the meaning of Nāgārjuna's *Fundamental Stanzas on the Middle Way*, the principal treatise of the Mādhyamika school of philosophy composed some four hundred years earlier. This work of Nāgārjuna is, in turn, essentially an attempt to clarify systematically the concept of voidness propounded in the Buddha's *Perfection of Wisdom* sutras.

Chandrakīrti's text comprises ten chapters, each of which corresponds to one of the ten bodhisattva spiritual levels (*bhūmi*). However, most of the chapters except the sixth are very brief, containing as few as one or two stanzas. They consist of a general description of the bodhisattva level as well as the practice of the particular perfection associated with it. The major portion of the text is taken up with a detailed discussion of the practice of the bodhisattva on the sixth spiritual level, i.e. the sixth perfection, the perfection of wisdom. This principally entails a probing logical analysis that aims at establishing the voidness of inherent existence of both phenomena in general and persons in particular. Frequently, this analytical method assumes the form of a dialectical critique of certain non-Buddhist as well as Buddhist schools that uphold the notion that phenomena, or certain phenomena, have an inherent self-existence.

What follows is a translation of the entire sixth chapter of Chandrakīrti's *Guide to the Middle Way*. The text is presented in prose form and has been clarified and explained according to the interpretation of Tsong Khapa as found in his commentarial work, the *Clear Illumination of the Intention*. The numbers alongside the text correspond to the original verse numbers. The paragraph formation has been made according to the topical outline of Tsong Khapa.

The translation of the text was brought to completion in 1980, in conjunction with oral explanations of Tsong Khapa's commentary given by Geshé Thubten Ngawang in the Tibetisches Zentrum, Hamburg. The sections in italics are the translator's gloss.

1 Introduction

1   The bodhisattva whose mind is placed evenly in the Approach, i.e. the sixth spiritual level, approaches the phenomenon of complete buddhahood; he sees the suchness of dependent arising; and, because he dwells in wisdom, he will achieve cessation.

2   Just as a person with good eyesight can easily lead many groups of blind people wherever they want to go, in this case too the mind of wisdom leads the virtues with defective eyesight, i.e. the other five perfections, and takes them to the very state of a conqueror.

3   Through both scriptural citation and reasoning, Nāgārjuna has clearly revealed this extremely profound phenomenon, suchness, in the same way as is understood by the bodhisattva on the Approach. Therefore, in the very way in which suchness has been explained in the textual tradition of the ārya Nāgārjuna, I shall likewise describe it here, in full accordance with that tradition.

4   Should an ordinary person hear about voidness and immediate-
5   ly experience the surging of such great joy that his eyes become moist with tears and the hairs on his body stand on end, such a person has the seed of the mind of complete buddhahood; he is a vessel to whom suchness, the truth perceived by the holy ones, should be revealed. In such a person the virtues that follow upon
6   hearing about voidness will arise: he will always adopt a perfect

moral discipline and adhere to it, bestow gifts, devote himself to compassion and cultivate patience. In order to liberate beings he will completely dedicate his wholesome deeds to awakening and 7 pay respect to the complete bodhisattvas. Such a person who is skilled in the ways of the profound and the vast will progressively achieve the spiritual level of Great Joy. Therefore, those who strive for that spiritual level should listen to this path.

2 The Selflessness of Phenomena

A. A REFUTATION OF PRODUCTION

8 An effect cannot arise from itself, but how could it come from something inherently other than itself? It cannot come from both, yet how could it exist without a cause?

1. Refutation of the Sāṃkhya doctrine of production from self
The non-Buddhist Sāṃkhya school maintains that a causal relation between two things could only be possible if the effect were in some way essentially identical with its cause. Without such identity there would be no grounds upon which to affirm any relationship. Therefore, they posit the view of production from self, i.e. production from a cause that is essentially identical to its effect. Chandrakīrti's principal objection to this view is that it would render any production of effects unnecessary. If the effect were essentially identical with its cause, what need would there be for it to be produced?

9 There is no point at all for something to arise from itself. It is also quite unreasonable for something that has been produced to be produced again. If it is maintained that a seed that has already been produced is later produced again, then the production of

such things as sprouts would never be found on this earth, and until the end of conditioned existence seeds alone would be abundantly produced. For how could the sprout ever come to destroy the seed?

One consequence of the Sāṃkhya doctrine of production from self would be that the shape, colour, taste, potency and ripening of a sprout could not be distinct from those of its creative cause, a seed. If, upon discarding the very nature it had before, a seed then becomes the nature of something other than itself, namely a sprout, how could it still have the nature of a seed? If the seed and the sprout are not of different natures, then just as the seed is not apprehended at the time of the sprout, likewise one should not apprehend the sprout. Alternatively, since they are of an identical nature, when one apprehends the sprout one should also apprehend the seed. Therefore, it is impossible to uphold this position of production from self.

Furthermore, even the people of the world do not maintain that a seed and a sprout have the same nature because they see the effects of a seed only when the cause itself has perished. Therefore, this firm conviction that things arise from themselves is unreasonable both in terms of suchness and in terms of the world.

When one asserts production from self, the product, the producer, the act and the agent all become identical. However, they are not identical. Therefore, one should not maintain this view of production from self, because in doing so the faults explained at length both here and in Nāgārjuna's *Fundamental Stanzas on Wisdom* will follow.

2. Refutation of production from other

In contrast to the Sāṃkhya doctrine of production from self, most Buddhist schools assert the otherness of, i.e. the essential difference between, a cause and its effect. If a cause and its effect were not inherently distinct from one another, there would, for them, be no grounds upon which to establish causal relationships. However, Chandrakīrti objects that causality is also rendered impossible in positing such a distinctness. If two phenomena were in their very

10

11

12

13

essence different from one another, how could they ever come to be connected by the invariable laws of causality?

a. *General refutation*

14   If an inherently other effect could arise in dependence upon inherently other causes, then the densest gloom should be able to arise even from flames. In fact, anything should be able to be produced from anything else, because even non-productive phenomena such as space are similar in their otherness.

15   However, the following objection may be raised: "A thing is called with certainty an effect only because something was actually able to create it. Likewise, that which had the ability to produce it — irrespective of its being other than the effect — is the cause. Moreover, because it must be produced from a seed that belongs to the same continuum as itself and is its producer, a rice sprout, for example, will never be produced from a grain of barley."

16   But because they are *other* than rice sprouts, such things as barley, stamens of flowers and evergreen trees (a) are not asserted to be the producers of rice sprouts, (b) do not have the ability to produce them, (c) do not belong to the same continuum as them and (d) are not at all similar to them. Likewise, because it too is said to be *other* than a rice-sprout, a rice seed could also conceivably lack those four qualities in relation to its sprout.

Otherness should be visible, as it is between two simultaneously

17   present people, but a sprout does not exist simultaneously with its seed because it does not exist until the seed has ceased to be evident. So when there is no otherness between them, how can a seed become other than a sprout? Thus the production of a sprout from a seed is not inherently established. And therefore, one should reject the position which states that one thing is produced from an inherently other thing.

18   Some may argue that just as the movements of the higher and lower pans of a balance are seen to be simultaneous, so are the production of the product and the cessation of the producer simultaneous.

Although the movement of the balance pans may be simultaneous, there is no such simultaneity in the case of a seed and a

sprout. For the sprout that is in the process of being produced is   19
yet to be produced and thus is not yet existent, whereas the seed
that is in the process of ceasing is asserted as an entity which is *yet*
to perish, and thus is still existent. So in that case how could the
production of a sprout from a seed be similar to the movement of
the pans of a balance? Moreover, without a sprout as the agent, i.e.
that in relation to which something else is determined to be an act,
the act of producing a sprout is not an entity that can be reason-
ably asserted.

If one considers visual consciousness to be simultaneous with its   20
producers, namely the eyes as well as the discernments and so
forth that arise in conjunction with them, then although it would
be quite other than those things, what would be the need for it to
arise into existence again? However, even if one now accepts that
an effect must be non-existent at the time of its causes, one should
still bear in mind the possible errors on this point as explained
above.

If the producer is a cause that produces a product other than   21
itself, one should consider whether the effect it produces is inherently existent, non-existent, both of these or neither. If the
effect were inherently existent, what need would there be of a
producer? And if it were non-existent, what could act as a cause
for it? Furthermore, what could act as a cause for something both
existent and non-existent? Likewise, what could act as a cause for
something neither existent nor non-existent?

We assert that the cognitions of people of the world are valid as   22
long as they remain within their own ordinary views. Therefore,
one might ask, what can be achieved through stating reasons to
prove this point of production from other. Surely the people of
the world understand that entities arise from entities other than
themselves. So what need is there for reasoning to prove the existence of production from other?

b. *A presentation of the two truths*

*In order to answer the above questions it is necessary to clarify the
precise extent of the validity of an ordinary person's cognition. This is
achieved through explaining the notion of the two truths.*

23   For all things two natures are apprehended: one found through seeing their reality and another found through seeing their deceptive character. The object of the mind that sees reality is suchness, i.e. the ultimate truth, and that of the mind that sees deceptive entities is the conventional truth.

24   Vision of deceptive entities is of two kinds: perception based upon non-defective senses and perception based on defective senses. The perceptions of those who have defective senses are regarded as mistaken in comparison with the perceptions of those

25   with good senses. Whatever is apprehended by the perceptions of one of the six senses not adversely affected by a cause for distortion is validly cognized by the world. But it is *true* for the world alone. Likewise, in terms of the world, everything else, e.g. a magician's illusion, is posited as mistaken.

26   A fundamental nature — in the way it is considered by the non-Buddhist Tīrthikas, who are entirely motivated by the sleep of nescience — is utterly non-existent, even in terms of the world. So too are such things as magician's illusions considered to be horses and mirages considered to be water.

27   Just as the non-existent objects seen by eyes affected with cataracts do not invalidate a consciousness unaffected with cataracts, similarly a mind devoid of stainless wisdom does not invalidate a stainless mind.

28   Because bewilderment obstructs one from seeing the nature of phenomena, it is said to be deceived. And the Mighty One taught that whatever objects are artificially affected by it and thus appear to be true are deceptive, i.e. conventional, truths. For those who have abandoned the apprehension of inherent existence, however, things which are so artificially affected are seen as merely deceptive but not as true.

29   Upon searching for fallacious entities such as the hairs seen by someone through the force of his cataracts, a person with good eyesight will see no hairs at all in the place where those very hairs are supposed to be. In a similar fashion should the perception of suchness be understood here.

30   If the perceptions of the world were valid cognitions of reality, the world would perceive suchness. In that case what would be

the need for the āryas to perceive it? What would be achieved by
the ārya's path? It is also unreasonable for the foolish to be
regarded as valid authorities on reality. In all respects the per-   31
ceptions of the world are invalid cognitions with regard to reality.
Therefore, when suchness is under consideration the views of the
world cannot contradict one. Nevertheless, simply because
something that is established in the world is well-known to the
world, one is contradicted by the world when one denies it.

Just because they inseminated their wives, the men of the world   32
announce, "I produced this son." And just because they sowed a
seed, they think, "I planted this tree." The notion of "production
from other" does not exist for the world.

At the time of the sprout there is no destruction of the seed, i.e.   33
no severance of its generic continuity, because the sprout is not
something inherently other than the seed. Nevertheless, at the
time of the sprout one cannot say that the seed exists, because the
sprout and the seed do not exist as one thing.

If the inherent characteristics of things were produced in depen-   34
dence upon causes and conditions, by denying those characteristics in the perception of voidness the things would thereby be
destroyed. Thus, the perception of voidness would become a
cause for the destruction of the nature of things. But such a notion
is unreasonable; therefore, inherent characteristics of things
cannot exist.

One should not analyze the nominal truths of the world to see   35
whether they are produced from self or other and so forth, because
when things such as forms and feelings are subjected to such
analysis, they are not found to exist in any way other than that of
having the nature of suchness.

When making an ultimate analysis of suchness, production   36
from both self and other is proved to be unreasonable. Likewise,
those very proofs show such production to be unreasonable even
nominally. Thus, what valid means of knowledge can establish
this inherent production?

Void, i.e. deceptive, things such as reflections are well known in   37
the world to arise in dependence upon a collection of causes and
conditions. And just as perceptions are produced from these void

38   reflections bearing their image, likewise, although all things are void of inherent characteristics, void effects are definitely produced from void causes.

    Moreover, the two truths are neither inherently permanent nor subject to annihilation, because they have no inherent nature.

39   An action does not inherently cease. Therefore, even without having recourse to such things as a foundation consciousness (*ālaya vijñāna*), effects are still able to arise from actions. Although, in certain cases, a long time may have elapsed since the action ceased, it should be understood that a corresponding effect will still occur.

40   Even when they are awake, foolish men continue to have desire for objects such as beautiful women that they saw in their dreams. Similarly, effects arise from actions which have ceased and have no inherent existence.

41   A person with cataracts sees the appearance of non-existent hairs and the like but he does not see the appearance of other things such as hares' horns and the offspring of barren women, even though those objects are equally non-existent. Likewise, it should be understood that although actions are equally devoid of inherent existence, those that have already come to fruition will not bear fruit again, whereas those that have not yet ripened will

42   produce effects. Therefore, it is seen that unpleasant ripening effects arise from black deeds and pleasant ripening effects from what is wholesome. However, he who perceives the lack of inherent existence of wholesome and unwholesome actions will be liberated from samsara. Thus analytical thought comes to a standstill when confronted with the relation between actions and their effects.

43   The doctrines that propound the existence of a foundation consciousness, the substantial existence of the person and that the aggregates alone are inherently existent, are intended by the Buddha for those who cannot at present understand the meaning of the profound truth of voidness that he explains.

44   Moreover, although the Buddha is free from the view of the transitory composite, i.e. the view of an inherently existent self, he still uses the terms "I" and "mine" in order to communicate the dharma to others. Likewise, although things have no inherent

nature, he may teach, in a way that is to be interpreted, that they do have such a nature. For he is able, by these means, to lead others gradually to the higher view of voidness.

c. *Refutation of the Chittamātra position*
The Chittamātra, or Mind-only, philosophy was initially formulated by the Buddhist sage Asaṅga in the third century A.D. Its principal contention is that all phenomena are in essence solely of the nature of mind. Therefore, they deny an external reality that is essentially distinct from the nature of mind. Unlike the Mādhyamika they do not interpret the concept of voidness as meaning the mere absence of inherent existence. On the contrary, they maintain that mind, as the basis of all phenomena, must inherently exist. The main thrust of Chandrakīrti's critique of the Chittamātra is aimed at showing the impossibility of establishing such an inherently existent mind.

i. *Refuting the notion of an inherently existent consciousness that has no external referent*
The Chittamātra school maintains that since there are no appre- 45
hensible objects of a substance other than mind, the bodhisattva abiding in wisdom, i.e. on the sixth spiritual level, does not see any subjective apprehensions which are of a nature other than them, and fully understands the three realms of existence to be merely consciousness. Therefore, he understands suchness to be merely consciousness. Just as waves emerge from the great ocean 46
when it is stirred by wind, so, for the Chittamātra, do dependent phenomena, which are merely consciousness, emerge through the ripening of potencies previously placed on the foundation con-sciousness, the common basis for the seeds of all things. Therefore, they assert that the inherently existent nature of 47
dependent phenomena should be accepted because they are the causes, i.e. the bases, for imputedly existent things. Furthermore, dependent phenomena arise from their own potencies without there being any external apprehensibles. They inherently exist and have the nature of not being the objects of any conceptual fabrication.

But what examples are there of a mind that inherently exists 48
without an external object? The Chittamātra might well give the

example of a dreaming mind. Now, this should be given some consideration. In our tradition, just as the object of the dream is non-existent, an inherently existent mind is also non-existent when one is dreaming. In that case, the inherently existent
49   dreaming mind that they give as their example could not exist. If, upon waking, such a mind is established as existent from one's recollection of the experience of the dream, external objects could likewise be established as existent. Because, just as one recollects "I saw . . .," and thereby establishes the existence of that mind, likewise the recollection of an external object in the dream should establish the existence of such an object.
50   However, the Chittamātra would argue that since visual perception is impossible during sleep, there can be no visual-forms existent at that time. Thus only mental consciousness can be existent. But, they would add, the aspect of what appears is mistakenly conceived to be externally existent. And just as consciousness occurs without any external objects during a dream, so does it occur now during the waking period.
51   In the same way that for them external objects are not produced during a dream, similarly the mind too is not inherently produced. During a dream the eyes, the visual objects and the perceptions
52   they produce are, all three of them, equally deceptive. Similarly the three components of auditory and other perceptual situations are also not inherently produced during dreams. And just as the objects, sense organs and perceptions in a dream are deceptive, so are all things deceptive now even while we are awake. The mind does not inherently exist; likewise, the experienced objects are non-inherently existent, and the sense organs too are not in-
53   herently produced. In this world, as long as people are asleep, the objects, sense-organs and perceptions of their dreams seem to them to exist in the same way as they do when they are awake. But upon waking they realize all three component elements of their dreams to have been non-existent. It is a similar experience when one wakes from the sleep of bewilderment.
A further example put forth by the Chittamātra is that of the perception of non-existent hairs that occurs for someone with cataracts. In this case they maintain that an inherently existent

perception occurs there without there being an external object. But this example is also invalid. The mind of someone whose eyes are affected by cataracts does perceive non-existent hairs through the force of his cataracts, and *in terms of his mind* the visual perception of those hairs and what it is that appear to be hairs are both true, i.e. existent. But for someone who sees things clearly, they are both deceptive. If an inherently existent perception of a non-existent object could exist for a person with cataracts, by directing our vision to the place where he sees non-existent hairs, we who have no cataracts should also perceive them because the non-existence of the object is the same for both of us. However, this does not happen. Therefore, an objectless, inherently existent perception cannot exist.

The Chittamātra explain that a perception of hairs does not occur for us because we who are looking in that place have no ripe potentials on our minds to see hairs there, not because an existent object of knowledge is absent. But since an inherently existent potential does not exist, such a perception cannot be established. Moreover, it is impossible that the potential for a particular perception could be present with that perception once it has been produced.

However, there can also exist no potential for something that is not yet produced. For when a quality, in this case the perception, is non-existent, there can exist no possessor of that quality, in this case the potential. If that were not the case, it would follow that the potential for the son of a barren woman could also exist. It may be asserted that one can speak of a potential for perception by referring to a perception that is in the process of coming to be. But since an inherently existent perception that is yet to be could *never* exist, its potential would be utterly non-existent. Furthermore, it may be argued that the perception that is coming to be and the potential for it exist in mutual dependence. But in that case the wise would proclaim them to have no inherent existence at all.

If a perception in the process of coming to be emerges from the ripening of a potential deposited by another perception that has already ceased, the resultant perception will be emerging from a

54

55

56

57

58

59

potential belonging to a perception inherently other than itself. According to the Chittamātra this would be so because in their successive emergence the individual instances of a continuum are inherently distinct from one another. Therefore, all things should be able to arise from all things that are other than themselves.

60   The Chittamātra would argue that this fault is not applicable, because although the individual instances of a continuum are inherently distinct, the instances do not possess distinct continuums, but are all instances of the same continuum. But this is something that remains to be proved, because in fact it is unreasonable for sequential entities that are inherently distinct to share the same

61   continuum. For example, the individual qualities of John and Bill are not included in the same continuum because they are quite distinct things belonging to different people. Likewise, it is unreasonable for all entities, which by their own characteristics are distinct from one another, to belong to the same continuum.

However, Chittamātrins may attempt to clarify their position as

62   follows: "The production of visual perception arises from its very own potential, which previously has been placed on the foundation consciousness, as soon as that potential ripens. However, in bewilderment, people recognize the physical eye-organ to be the basis that has the potential for the visual perception. In fact, there

63   exists no eye-organ distinct from consciousness. In this world people maintain that the mind apprehends external objects because they do not understand that perceptions that arise from sense organs occur as simple "blue-awareness" and so forth from the ripening of their own seeds, which have been placed on the foundation consciousness, not from the apprehension of anything

64   external. While dreaming, a perception bearing the aspect of a material form arises from the ripening of its own potential without there being a distinct material object present. Similarly, during this waking state too, perception exists without there being any external objects."

65   But just as mental perceptions that behold objects such as blue colours occur in the dream state without the assistance of an eye-organ, likewise why can they not be produced from the ripening

of the seeds of mental perception for awake blind people, who also have no functioning eye-organs? If, as the Chittamātra assert, the ripening of the potential for such mental perceptions exists while one is dreaming but ceases to exist when one is awake, then just as the ripening of the potential for mental perceptions that behold forms and so forth is non-existent for the blind during the waking state, why would it be unreasonable to say that it is non-existent during the dream state? Just as the lack of eyes is not the cause for the ripening of the potential that enables a blind person to see forms while awake, likewise in the dream state, sleep cannot be the cause for the ripening of the potential to see forms. Therefore, even in the dream state, we maintain that things such as forms are the causes for the deceptive perceptions of forms, and that dream-eyes are also causes for such perceptions.

No matter what replies the Chittamātrins give us, we see their basic theses to be equally incapable of proof. Thus the arguments of this school are dispelled. The refutation of their system is also not in contradiction with scriptural authority, because the buddhas have never declared that things inherently exist.

Furthermore, a ground covered with skeletons, which is beheld by the yogī who is following the instructions of his guru to meditate on the foul aspect of the body, is also beheld without inherent production of the object, the sense-organ and the perception, because it is taught that such a concentration is a mistaken state of attention, i.e. one that does not apprehend suchness. If that perception of skeletons inherently existed, whatever appeared to it would have to exist in the way it appeared. Thus, the perception would be a state of attention which apprehends suchness. If, according to the Chittamātra, the objects of the mind contemplating the foul are just like the objects of all sensory perception, then, should someone else who is not a yogī direct his mind to the place where the yogī is meditating, he also should perceive skeletons there. And in that case, the concentration of the yogī could no longer be considered false, i.e. as a mistaken state of attention. Moreover, a ghost's valid perception of a stream of running water's being pus would have to be equated with the

66

67

68

69

70

71

invalid perceptions of someone whose eyes are affected by cataracts.

In short, the point to be understood is this: just as the objects of consciousness have no inherent existence, neither does the mind have any inherent existence.

ii. *Refuting the notion of apperception, a self-cognizing aspect of consciousness that the Chittamātra assert in order to establish inherently existent dependent entities*

72   If there exist such things as dependent entities that, since there are no external objects to apprehend, are separate from being apprehensions that are essentially other than external objects, and thus are void of being either apprehensibles or apprehensions that are substantially distinct from one another, what consciousness can know of their existence? One cannot say that they exist without

73   being apprehended by consciousness, and it cannot be established, as the Chittamātra maintain, that they are experienced by themselves through apperception (*rang.rig*).

It is claimed that apperception is established from recollections that occur at a later time. But the unestablished inherently existent recollections that the Chittamātra speak of in order to prove an as yet unestablished apperception are no proof at all for

74   apperception. For even if apperception were established, it would still be unreasonable for the memory to recollect the objects of a previous apperception. Why? Because it is maintained that the later recollection and the previous object of apperception are inherently other phenomena. This would be like the memory recollecting something one never experienced. This argument, "because they are inherently other," effectively eliminates any possibility of inclusion within one continuum, or of causal relationship (59).

75   For us a recollection does not exist as inherently other than the consciousness that previously experienced the object. Thus one simply recollects, "I saw . . . ." This is the way it conventionally occurs in the world, i.e. unencumbered by philosophical considerations.

76   Therefore, if apperception does not exist, what consciousness is

there to apprehend the dependent entities asserted by the Chittamātra? Since the three components of any action — the agent, the acted upon and the act — can never be one undifferentiated entity, it is not reasonable for consciousness to apprehend itself.

Although it may be asserted that there exist things established 77 by their own nature that are inherently unproduced and unknown to valid cognition, the existence of such things cannot be proven by any reasoning. So how can the offspring of barren women have any effect at all on those who maintain the Chittamātra position?

When dependent entities such as consciousness do not have a 78 trace of inherent existence, how can they be the cause, i.e. the substantial basis, for conventional phenomena? By being attached like the Chittamātra to the inherent existence of mere consciousness as the substance of dependent entities, all that is commonly known in the world breaks down.

Those who remain outside the path shown by the venerable 79 master Nāgārjuna lack the principal means for attaining peace. For they fail to uphold effectively the distinction between conventional truths and the truth of suchness. And because of this failure they will not find liberation. Why is this so? Because a 80 flawless presentation of nominal, or conventional, truths is the means for a correct understanding of ultimate truth and thus an understanding of ultimate truth arises from those means. But those who do not know how to distinguish between these two truths enter upon an unfortunate course because of their mistaken conceptions.

We do not accept even as *conventional* truths the inherently 81 existent dependent entities that the Chittamātra assert. However, for the sake of leading others to the goal, we sometimes say to the world that the aggregates and so forth inherently exist, whereas in fact they have no inherent existence. If conventional phenomena 82 were non-existent for the world in the same way as they are non-existent for arhats who have discarded their aggregates and entered the peace of nirvana, then, just as we would not say that such phenomena existed for those arhats, we would also not say that they existed for the world. If the Chittamātra think that they 83 are not contradicted by the world, let them go and deny to the people of the world conventionally accepted phenomena such as external existence. Let us see them and the world argue on these points. After this debate we shall rely upon whoever shows himself to be the stronger.

iii. *The word "only" in the term "Mind-only" (Chittamātra) does not deny the existence of external phenomena*

84   The bodhisattva on the Approach who is nearing the sphere of reality is said to understand the three worlds to be consciousness, i.e. mind, only. He has realized that a permanent self is not the creator of the world and therefore now understands mind alone to be the creator.

85   In order to further develop the minds of the intelligent, the Omniscient One made, in the *Descent into Laṅkā Sutra*, certain adamantine proclamations destroying the high mountain peaks of the non-Buddhists' wrong views. These statements serve to
86   clarify the meaning he intended with the notion "mind-only." In some of their treatises, the non-Buddhists claim that such things as a person are the creator of the aggregates and so forth. It was upon seeing that such things are not the creator that the Conqueror declared mind alone to be the creator of the world.

87   Just as the Awakened One (Buddha) is so called from his being awakened to suchness, likewise, while meaning that between mind and form only mind is of principal importance, the notion "mind-only" is taught to the world in some sutras. But it is not the aim of those sutras to deny thereby the external existence of form
88   and to assert that mind alone is inherently existent. According to the Chittamātra, in the *Ten Grounds Sutra* the Buddha denies the existence of external forms on the basis of his understanding that the three worlds are only inherently existent mind. If this were so, why, in the same sutra, does the Magnanimous One go on to say that mind is produced from bewilderment and actions and is thus
89   dependently and not inherently existent? Moreover, the mind itself creates living beings and constructs the various worlds in which they live. It is also taught that every form of life is produced from actions; but without the mind those actions would not exist.

Indeed form exists; but unlike mind, it does not exist as the creator   90
of life. Therefore, although we deny that there is a creator other
than mind, we do not deny that external forms exist.

For those who dwell amidst the realities of the world, *all* the five   91
aggregates, both mental and physical, exist because they are
commonly known to the world. But for the yogī who assents to
what appears to the wisdom that directly cognizes suchness,
none of the five aggregates occur. Therefore, if one asserts the non-   92
existence of external forms, one should not maintain that mind
exists; and if one asserts the existence of mind, one should not
maintain that external forms are non-existent. In the *Perfection of
Wisdom Sutras* the Buddha denied equally the inherent existence
of mind *and* form, whereas in the *Abhidharma* he affirmed equally
the characteristics of each. Even were these two levels of truth to   93
perish, the substantially existent dependent entities of the
Cittamātra would not be established because they would still be
refuted by our previous arguments. Therefore, as has been
progressively explained above, one should understand that pri-
mordially things are ultimately unproduced, although in terms of
worldly convention they are produced.

Furthermore, it is said in the *Descent into Laṅkā Sutra* that   94
externally appearing entities do not exist; rather, it is the mind
that appears as all those diverse forms. But this is taught in order
to turn away from forms those who are extremely attached to
them. The meaning of the statement is to be interpreted. Such   95
passages as this were not only said by the Teacher to be of an interpretative meaning, but can be proved to be such by reasoning.
Moreover, this passage makes it clear that other sutras which take
a similar position are also to be interpreted and not taken literally.

The buddhas have also said that if the non-existence of   96
externally existent objects of consciousness is taught first, it will
be easier subsequently to discover the absence of inherently
existent consciousness. Thus, first externally existent objects of
consciousness should be negated because, if their non-existence is
understood, the refutation of consciousness, i.e. the understanding of its selflessness, can be easily realized.

Hence one should understand that some statements are to be   97 interpreted whereas others are to be taken literally. Sutras whose subject matter deals with what is not actually suchness are said to be of interpretative meaning; having understood them to be so we should interpret them accordingly. Sutras whose subject matter deals explicitly with voidness are said to be of definitive meaning and thus we should take them literally.

3. *Refutation of production from both self and other*

98   Production from both self and other together is not something reasonable because the faults of production from self or other individually, which we explained above, would be just as applicable to production from self and other together. Such a mode of production neither exists in the world nor can be asserted as suchness for the simple reason that neither production from self nor from other can be individually established.

4. *Refutation of the Hedonist (Chārvāka) doctrine of production from no cause*

99   If it were the case that things are produced from no cause at all, all things could always be produced from anything else. In that case people in the world would not have to undergo the many hardships of gathering seeds and so forth in order to produce their
100   crops. If living beings were devoid of causes they would be simply inapprehensible, like the scent and the colour of a sky-lotus. But because these extremely diverse beings *are* apprehensible, one should understand them to be produced from their own causes, just as one's own perception of blueness, for example, arises in dependence upon a blue patch of colour.
101   If the four material elements of earth, water, fire and air do not have the nature of being the ultimate suchness — i.e. the nature ascribed to them in the Chārvāka scriptures and thus the way that the Chārvākas perceive them — how, when there exists such darkness in the mind concerning such gross things, can the Chārvākas correctly understand the very subtle phenomenon of
102   future lives? Moreover, when they deny the existence of future lives, they have a mistaken understanding of the nature of a

knowable phenomenon, because they take the physical body as the correlate upon the basis of which they put forth such views. This is likewise the case when they assert the inherently existent nature of the elements. However, we have already explained how the elements have no inherent existence, for we have now refuted in general production from self, from other, from both self and other together and from no cause. Thus the elements, although they were not specifically mentioned above, can be understood to have no inherent existence.

103

B. *CONCLUDING REMARKS*

Since they are not produced from self, from other, from both self and other and are not independent of any causes, all things are devoid of inherent existence.

104

The people of the world are subject to great bewilderment as dense as a mass of clouds, hence the nature of objects appears to them in a mistaken way. Through the force of their cataracts some people mistakenly see hairs where in fact there are none, two moons in the sky, and imaginary peacock feathers, flies and so forth. Similarly, through the power of the fallacious character of bewilderment, ordinary unwise people cognize a variety of conditioned phenomena with their minds. When the Buddha taught that formative actions arise in dependence upon bewildered ignorance but do not occur without that bewilderment, it was certainly intended that this be so understood only by the unwise. But the wise, whose noble sun-like minds dispel the dense gloom of ignorance, upon hearing such teachings only experience the voidness of inherent existence of conditioned phenomena and thereby are liberated from samsara.

105

106

It might be thought that if things did not ultimately, i.e. inherently, exist, they could not exist conventionally either, like the son of a barren woman. Therefore, it may be concluded, they must exist inherently, by their own nature.

107

To begin with one should, for a while, argue only with those who have cataracts: "Since the hairs which appear to you are unproduced, why do you not also see sons of barren women, for they

108

too are unproduced?" Only later should one bring such analysis to bear on the condition of those whose perceptions are distorted by
109   the cataracts of ignorance. One should ask of them: "If you can see such unproduced things as houses in your dreams, cities of gandharvas, the water of a mirage, the illusory creations of a magician and a face in a reflection, why do you say that it is un-reasonable to see the son of a barren woman, which is as non-
110   existent as them?" Therefore, although forms and so forth are likewise unproduced, unlike the son of a barren woman they are not invisible to the people of the world. Hence the objection raised above — that if things did not ultimately exist they could not be seen even conventionally, like the son of a barren woman — is not justified.

111   The inherent production of the son of a barren woman exists neither ultimately nor for the world, i.e. conventionally. Similarly, all things are not inherently produced either ultimately or for the
112   world. Therefore, the Teacher has said that all phenomena are pacified from the very beginning, they lack inherent production and by their very nature are completely beyond sorrow (lit: in
113   nirvana). Hence inherent production never takes place. Things such as jugs do not ultimately exist yet they are well known to the world and thus conventionally exist. All things in fact exist in this way; thus it does not follow that just because they are ultimately non-existent they are similar to the offspring of barren women.

114   Things are not produced without causes, nor from causes such as Ishvara, nor from self, other, or both self and other together.
115   Therefore, they can be produced only *dependently*. And since things arise only dependently, these conceptions that they arise from self, other and so forth are unable to understand the matter correctly. Hence the entire fabric of evil views is cut to pieces by
116   the reasoning of dependent arising. Only if things are appre-hended as inherently existent do such conceptions come about. But we have made a thorough analysis which has determined how things do *not* inherently exist. Thus when an apprehension of in-herently existent things is absent, those conceptions will not occur, as, for example, without fuel there will be no fire.
117   Ordinary beings, i.e. those who do not understand voidness, are

bound by their extreme conceptions, but the yogī who has gained a non conceptual insight into voidness is thereby liberated. Therefore, the wise have taught that the goal of the Mādhyamika analysis is a reversal of conception that comes about through an utter negation of whatever is apprehended by extreme conceptions. Nāgārjuna did not compose his treatises on Mā- 118
dhyamaka because of an attachment to logical analysis and polemic. He taught suchness in order to lead others to liberation. However, there is no contradiction if, in explaining suchness, the ideas expounded in the texts of others are refuted through logical analysis and argument. Nevertheless, any attachment to one's 119
own views and likewise any aversion to the views of others are simply conceptions that keep one in bondage. Therefore, dispel such attachment and anger and use analysis for the swift attainment of liberation.

3 The Selflessness of the Person

Having refuted the notion of inherent existence in general, Chandrakīrti now turns his attention to an analysis of the person in particular. It is the understanding of the voidness of inherent existence of the person that has the greatest initial effect in uprooting unwholesome modes of thought and behaviour.

120   The yogī perceives that all the disturbing conceptions and negative aspects of existence arise from the view of the transitory composite (*'jig.lta*), i.e. the disturbing conception of an inherently existent I and mine. Upon understanding the self to be an objective referent of this view, he proceeds to negate such an inherently existent self.

A. *REFUTATION OF AN INHERENTLY EXISTENT "I"*

1. *Refutation of the self posited by non-Buddhists to be essentially distinct from the aggregates*

121   The non-Buddhist Sāṃkhya school considers the self to be the experiencer of pleasure and pain, something permanent, not a creator, devoid of the qualities, (i.e. *sattva*, *rajaḥ* and *tamaḥ*) and inactive. The other non-Buddhist traditions, such as the

Vaisheshika school, differ from the Sāṃkhya school as well as from one another according to various slight distinctions they make concerning the specific qualities of the self.

However, such a self is non-existent because it is unproduced, like the son of a barren woman. It is also unreasonable for it to be the basis for the innate apprehension of I. Even conventionally it cannot be asserted to exist. All the characteristics of that self, which are described by the non-Buddhists in their various scriptures, are refuted by reason of their non-production, a quality that they themselves attribute to the self. Hence, all those characteristics are non-existent. Therefore, there exists no self that is essentially other than the aggregates because, apart from apprehensions of the aggregates, no apprehension of an independent self can be established. Furthermore, such a self is not even asserted as the basis, i.e. the referent, of the world's innate apprehension of I because the world still has a view of the self even though it does not know of the self posited by non-Buddhist philosophers. Likewise, beings who have spent many aeons as animals also do not behold an unproduced and permanent self, although it is clear that they are involved in the apprehension of a self-identity. Thus there can be no self at all existing as something other than the aggregates.

2. *Refutation of certain Buddhist schools who regard the aggregates to be the self*

Some Buddhists maintain that because the self is not established as essentially other than the aggregates, the aggregates alone must be the referent for the view of the self, i.e. the view of the transitory composite. Certain adherents of the Saṃmitīya school, for example, assert all five aggregates to be the basis, i.e. the referent, for the view of the self, whereas other adherents of this school assert the mind alone to be the self.

But, if the aggregates were the self, since they are many, one person would have many selves. Furthermore, since the aggregates are substances, the self too would have to be a substance. In that case, the view of the transitory composite would

122

123

124

125

126

127

128   apprehend a substance and therefore, just like a perception of blue or yellow, it would not be mistaken. Moreover, upon passing into the state of non-residual nirvana, the self would definitely cease, because it is asserted by some Buddhist schools that at this time the five aggregates cease. But at the moments prior to the attainment of nirvana the self would inherently arise and perish just like the aggregates. Furthermore, upon perishing the agent would cease to exist and therefore there would be no basis upon which the impressions of an action could remain. In that case there could be no results of an action. Alternatively, the results of an action accumulated by one person would be experienced by someone else.

129   One may reply that there is no contradiction here as long as it is asserted that ultimately the individual instances exist in one continuum. But in our previous analyses (60-61) we explained the logical faults in the notion of such a continuum. Therefore, it is unreasonable to assert that the aggregates or the mind are the self.

Furthermore, the Buddha refused to comment on certain questions such as, "Does the world have an end?" Therefore, to assert that the aggregates are the self would imply that the Buddha committed himself on certain points (such as whether the tathāgata continues after death or not) when in fact he did not.

130   In the view of these Buddhists, a yogī who directly perceives the absence of a self would definitely perceive the absence of things, i.e. the aggregates, too. However, they themselves would not accept this. They would reply that when he perceived the absence of a self, he rejected, i.e. perceived the absence of, a *permanent* self. Thus it would follow that the mind and the

131   aggregates could not be the self. Hence, in their view, a yogī who perceived the absence of a self did not understand the suchness of such things as forms. Therefore, he would apprehend forms and so forth as inherently existent. In that case, attachment towards those things could still occur because he would lack an understanding of their nature.

132   It may be asserted that the aggregates are the self because the Teacher himself taught that the aggregates are the self. However, in those instances the Buddha was denying that there is a self that

is essentially other than the aggregates because, in other sutras, he stated that form and the other aggregates are *not* the self. He declared quite clearly that forms and feelings are not the self; neither are discernments, formative elements or consciousness. Therefore, we can conclude that he did not assert the aggregates to be the self. 133

It might be argued that when the aggregates are described as the self, what is actually meant is that the *collection* of the aggregates is the self, not the individual aggregates themselves. However, the self is also spoken of as the "master," the "controller" and the "witness" — but a mere collection can be neither a master, controller nor witness, because it has no substantial existence. Therefore, the self cannot be the collection of the aggregates. 134

In this case, it would be like saying that the piled-up collection of the parts of a cart could be the cart itself. This would follow since a cart and the self would be similar in their being posited as the collection of their parts. 135

Moreover, in some sutras it is taught that the self is imputed in *dependence upon* the collection of the aggregates. Therefore, the mere collection of the aggregates cannot be the self.

Some would say that the shape of the aggregates is the self. In that case one could only call the material elements the self, because they alone have shape; the collection of the mental elements could not be posited as the self, because they are devoid of any shape. 136

It is unreasonable for the grasper, i.e. the self, to be something which is identical with what it grasps, i.e. the aggregates. In that case the agent and what is acted upon would become identical. This would be equivalent to identifying a potter with his pot. It would be fallacious then to imagine that the agent, i.e. the self, is non-existent, whereas what is acted upon, i.e. the aggregates, exists: if there is no agent, there can also be nothing that is acted upon. 137

In the *Meeting of Father and Son Sutra* the Buddha taught clearly that the self is dependent upon the six elements — earth, water, fire, air, consciousness and space — and the six bases — the sense fields of visual, auditory, olfactory, gustatory, tactile and 138

139 mental contact. Likewise he stated that the self is imputed in dependence upon the phenomena of the mind and the mental events, which are apprehended as the basis for that imputation. Therefore, the self is neither the various elements individually nor their mere collection. And the mind that instinctively apprehends I does *not* refer to them.

140 Some maintain that when the lack of self is understood one merely rejects, i.e. perceives the lack of, a permanent self. But they do not assert that this permanent self is the basis for the innate apprehension of I. Therefore, it is most peculiar to say that this knowledge of the lack of a permanent self can uproot the

141 primordial view of self. Imagine a frightened person who has noticed a snake living in a hole in the wall of his house. Others would simply laugh at him if he tried to dispel his fear of the snake by thinking, "There is no elephant in my house."

3. *Refutation of other misconceptions concerning the nature of the relationship between the self and the aggregates*

142 The self does not exist in inherent dependence upon the aggregates and neither do the aggregates exist in inherent dependence upon the self. Only if the self and the aggregates were essentially other could such conceptions be correct. But because such an inherent otherness does not exist, these conceptions are mistaken.

143 The self is not asserted to inherently possess form because it does not exist as either inherently identical with or distinct from form. Therefore, there exists no inherent relationship of possession between the self and the aggregates. A person can possess something essentially other than himself, such as a cow, and he can possess something that is not essentially other than himself, such as form. But it is impossible for the self inherently to possess form, because it is neither identical with nor other than form.

144 Therefore, form is not the self; the self does not inherently possess form; the self does not inherently exist in form; and form does not inherently exist in the self. Likewise, these four aspects of the view of the transitory composite should be understood with regard to the other four aggregates. Thus we assert twenty views

of the self. The thunderbolt of understanding selflessness shatters   145
the mountain of views about the self. And together with the view
of the self are destroyed these twenty high peaks that rise up out of
the huge mountain of the view of the transitory composite.

4. *Refutation of the notion of a substantially existent self that is neither identical with nor other than the aggregates*

Some adherents of the Saṃmitīya school assert the person, i.e. the   146
self, to be substantially existent yet indescribable. For them it
cannot be spoken of as either identical with or other than the
aggregates, neither permanent nor impermanent and so forth.
However, they also assert it to be an object known by the six
senses, as well as the basis for the apprehension of I.

Just as one does not regard the mind's relation to the body as in-   147
describable, it is incomprehensible how the relation between any
substantially existent things can be indescribable. If the self were
substantially existent, then being something just like the mind it
could not be indescribable in relation to the aggregates. It would   148
follow for these Saṃmitīyas that a jug, the nature of which they
regard as not being a self-sufficient thing, would be indescribable
in relation to its parts such as its form. Therefore, they should not
regard this self, which they claim to be indescribable in relation to
the aggregates, as existing by its own nature. They assert that con-   149
sciousness is not other than itself but that it is something other
than such things as form. Thus they definitely see these two
aspects of identity and difference among things. Therefore, the
self they posit cannot exist substantially because it is devoid of the
qualities of being identical or different that characterize all things.

5. *Showing how the self is merely a dependent imputation by referring to the analogy of the cart*

Hence the basis for the apprehension of I is not something   150
inherently existent. The self is neither essentially other than the
aggregates nor of the nature of the aggregates. It is not the basis of
the aggregates nor does it inherently possess them. Rather, the self
is established in dependence upon the aggregates. In this respect it   151

is similar to a cart, for a cart is not asserted either (1) to be essentially other than its parts, or (2) to be identical with them, or (3) inherently to possess them, or (4) to be inherently dependent upon them, or (5) to be the basis upon which they inherently depend, or (6) to be the mere collection of them, or (7) to be their shape.

152   If the mere collection of the parts were the cart, the collection of the same parts placed in a heap should also be the cart.

Some Buddhist schools maintain that not the cart but the collection of its parts is the part-bearer. But if the part-bearer is not the cart, the parts will also not be it. Therefore, it is also unreasonable for the mere shape, as well as for the mere collection of the parts, to be the cart.

153   However, some people do assert that the mere shape of the parts is the cart. First, let us assume that the shape of the individual parts prior to the assemblage of the cart exists in the same way as it does when the parts are subsequently assembled into a cart. Since the shape of the parts is not the cart when the parts are dispersed, there is no reason for them to be the cart when they are assembled.

154   Now, if when assembled as a cart, the wheels and so forth have a shape different from the shape they had before, such a difference should be observable visually. However, it is not. Therefore, the

155   mere shape of the individual parts cannot be the cart. According to such people, a substantially existent collection does not exist in the slightest. Hence for them the shape cannot be imputed upon the basis of the collection of the parts, because they believe that a basis for imputation must be substantially existent. So how, when it depends upon something that has no substantial existence, could the shape which is posited as the cart even be seen?

156   According to their assertion of the non-substantial existence of the collection, they should understand that *all* effects with an untrue nature are produced in dependence upon causes which are

157   also untrue. It is likewise unreasonable to maintain, as many Buddhist schools do, that, since the qualities of form and so forth when placed in a particular way constitute the jug, a perception of a jug occurs with regard to them. Furthermore, since their lack of inherent *production* has now been explained, forms and so forth must also lack inherent *existence*. For this reason too it is unreason-

able for substantially existent jugs to be the shape of the forms and so forth which are their parts.

Indeed, through this seven-fold analysis (151), the cart is found to be established neither ultimately nor in terms of worldly convention. However, *without* such analysis it is, in accordance with the conventions of the world, imputed in dependence upon its parts. 158

In the world it is acknowledged that a cart *has* parts and *has* pieces. It is likewise said that a cart *possesses* those parts. Furthermore, in relation to the bodies and minds that they possess, people are also established as possessors. One should not destroy these conventional phenomena well known in the world. 159

Something which cannot be found through the seven-fold analysis cannot be said to exist inherently. Thus the yogī does not find the very existence of the cart and in this way he easily penetrates suchness. However, it should be asserted here that, without analysis, the cart *is* established. 160

If the cart does not inherently exist, the part-possessor is not inherently existent. Therefore, the parts too cannot inherently exist. If, for example, the cart were burned, its parts would also cease to exist. Likewise, when the inherent existence of the part-possessor is burned away by the mental fire of wisdom, so is the inherent existence of the parts consumed. 161

Similarly, on the basis of what is well known in the world, we maintain that the self too depends upon the aggregates, the elements and the six sense-fields and, just like the cart, is the possessor of its parts. In this case the aggregates and so forth, which are possessed, are the objects of the act of possession, and self is the agent of possession. 162

Once the self has been posited as a dependent imputation it cannot be established as the basis for any extreme conceptions. Thus such conceptions are easily dismissed. The self is not an inherently existent thing. Therefore, it is neither inherently stable nor unstable, neither inherently produced nor destroyed, neither inherently identical with nor distinct from the aggregates, and neither inherently permanent nor impermanent and so forth. 163

The self in reference to which the mind that apprehends I 164 constantly arises in sentient beings and in reference to whose possessions the mind that apprehends mine occurs is, in terms of what is well known and unanalyzed, established by bewilderment, not by its own intrinsic nature.

B. *REFUTATION OF AN INHERENTLY EXISTENT MINE*

165   There exist no objects of action for an agent who does not exist. Therefore, an inherently existent mine cannot exist when there is no inherently existent self. Hence the yogī who beholds the voidness of an inherently existent self and mine is liberated from samsara.

C. *CONCLUDING REMARKS*

166   Things such as jugs, cloth, tents, armies, forests, rosaries, trees, houses, trolleys and guest-houses should be understood to exist in the way they are commonly spoken of by people because the
167   Buddha did not argue with the world over these matters. Furthermore, by applying the analysis of the cart to part-possessors and their parts, quality-possessors and their qualities, people with attachment and their desires, bases of characteristics and their characteristics and fire and the fuel it burns, one finds that they do not exist in any of the seven ways. But as long as they are not subjected to such analysis, they do exist in another way: namely, in terms of their being well known to the world.
168   Only if a cause has produced a product can it be a cause. But if a result has not been produced, since production is lacking there can be no causes for it. Likewise for results: they can only be produced when their causes exist. Therefore, cause and result are *mutually* dependent. Now, if they inherently existed, which would arise in dependence upon the other? And which would
169   precede the other? If causes inherently produced results, would they be contiguous with their results or not? If they were contiguous with the results they produced, cause and result would become one identical force. One would then be unable to dis-

tinguish between them, because the producer and its result would no longer be distinct. But, on the other hand, if they were distinct and not contiguous, that which was asserted to be the cause for a particular result would really be no different from whatever else was not its cause. There are no other ways to conceive of this phenomenon once these two alternatives have been eliminated. Therefore, an inherently existent cause could not produce any results. Hence, what are called "results" have no inherent existence and, since there is no reason for positing something as a cause when it has produced no results, causes too have no inherent existence. Both cause and result are similar to a magician's illusion in their not being inherently produced. Therefore, for us these problems of contiguity and so forth do not arise. We simply accept as existent whatever things are well known in the world.

170

However, the following argument may be raised: "But what about the refutation stated above? Does it effect its refutation through being contiguous with what it refutes or not? Do not exactly the same faults apply to the Mādhyamikas themselves? In pronouncing their refutations they only destroy their own position. Thus they are unable to refute the positions of others that they claim to refute. With fallacious arguments, the consequences of which are equally applicable to their own pronouncements, they quite illogically deny and negate everything. Therefore, no wise or saintly people would ever assert what they do. Since they have no position of their own, they are merely engaged in sophistry."*

171

172

This objection, "Does the refutation effect its refutation through being contiguous with what it refutes or not?" would only be applicable to someone who has a definite position, i.e. someone who asserts inherent existence. But we do not have such a position. It is therefore impossible to ascribe such logical consequences to us.

173

At the time of an eclipse one can observe what is happening to the shape of the sun by looking at its reflection. Yet although it is illogical to say that the sun and its reflection are either contiguous

174

*Here, one engaged in sophistry is defined as someone who takes no position of his own and only criticizes the positions of others. (*sun.ci.phyin.du.rgol.ba*)

175   or not contiguous, nevertheless, merely through the power of convention one can affirm that the reflection arises in dependence upon the sun. Even though a reflection is not true it can still establish whether or not one's face is clean. Thus it is capable of performing a function. Likewise here, although our reasoning may lack any inherent validity, it is seen to be capable of cleaning the face of wisdom. One should recognize that it can lead to an understanding of what we are trying to prove: the lack of any inherent nature.

176   The logical objections of contiguity and so forth would be applicable to us only if we were to maintain that the nature of the reasoning — that which gives rise to the understanding of what is proved — and the nature of that which is actually understood — that which is proved — were inherently existent. But we assert that they have no inherent existence. Therefore, the objections our critics make against us are utterly in vain.

177   One can very easily gain the understanding that all things lack an inherent thingness. But for others, such as ourselves, a similar comprehension of an inherent nature in things is not at all easy to gain for the simple reason that such an inherent nature is unfindable. So why, when the people of the world request one's help, should one entangle them in a web of harmful ideation?

178   First one should understand these additional refutations of the Realist position given above (168-170). Having done so one should then reject the arguments that we stated (171-172) in order to present the answers that the opponents gave to our objections of contiguity and so forth. By no means are we merely engaged in sophistry; the additional refutations stated above are for the sake of our opponents' own understanding.

4 The Divisions of Voidness

It must be emphasized that in classifying voidness the author is not speaking of qualitatively different forms of voidness but of different bases, i.e. internal entities, external entities etc., to which the characteristic of voidness applies. Voidness itself, i.e. the lack of inherent existence, does not differ in quality from one object to another.

In order to lead beings of different capacities to liberation, the Buddha taught two kinds of selflessness: the selflessness of phenomena and the selflessness of persons. The Teacher further divided these two selflessnesses into many different kinds in accordance with the varied inclinations of his disciples. In an extensive classification he spoke of sixteen voidnesses; in a more concise form he spoke of just four. He also regarded these voidnesses as the great vehicle.

A. THE SIXTEEN VOIDNESSES

1. The voidness of internal entities

The eye is void of being an inherently existent eye because its very nature is that of being void of inherent existence. The ears, the nose, the tongue, the body and the mind are also described in a

182　similar way. All these things are void because ultimately they
neither remain fixed and static nor do they perish. This very lack
of inherent existence of the six senses is regarded as the voidness
of internal entities.

2. *The voidness of external entities*

183　Visual-forms are void of being inherently existent visual-forms
because their very nature is that of being void. Sounds, smells,
tastes, tactile sensations and mental phenomena should be under-
184　stood in the same way. The very lack of inherent existence of
visual-forms and so forth is asserted to be the voidness of external
entities.

3. *The voidness of the internal and external*

The lack of inherent existence of those entities that are both
internal and external, such as the gross physical bases of the
senses, is the voidness of the internal and external.

4. *The voidness of voidness*

185　The wise call the lack of inherent existence of such phenomena
voidness. But they also maintain that this voidness too is void of
186　being an inherently existent voidness. This voidness of the so-
called voidness is regarded as the voidness of voidness. The
Buddha spoke of this in order to counteract the tendency of the
mind to apprehend voidness as inherently existent.

5. *The voidness of immensity*

187　The directions are immense because they pervade every single
physical world as well as the sentient beings who abide there and
because, by taking their immeasurability as an example, the four
immeasurable states of love and so forth are thus regarded as
188　boundless. Therefore, the voidness of inherent existence of these
ten directions is the voidness of immensity. It is taught in order to
counteract the tendency of apprehending the directions as inherently immense.

6. *The voidness of the ultimate*

189　Here the ultimate means nirvana because nirvana is the supreme necessity. Thus the voidness of inherent existence of nirvana is the voidness of the ultimate. The Knower of the Ultimate, i.e. the Buddha, likewise taught the voidness of the ultimate in order to counteract the tendency of the mind to apprehend nirvana as an inherently existent thing.

7. *The voidness of the conditioned*
The three worlds are declared to be conditioned because they arise from causal conditions. And their voidness of inherent existence is taught as the voidness of the conditioned.

8. *The voidness of the unconditioned*
Phenomena that lack production — i.e. the quality of changing into something else once they have come into existence — and impermanence — i.e. destructability — are unconditioned. Their voidness of inherent existence is the voidness of the unconditioned.

9. *The voidness of that which is beyond extremes*
Whatever lacks the extremes of permanence and annihilation is described as being beyond extremes. Its mere voidness of inherent existence is called the voidness of that which is beyond extremes.

10. *The voidness of that which has neither beginning nor end*
Samsara is described as having neither beginning nor end because it has no first beginning and no final end. The scriptures declare that the sheer absence of inherent existence of this state of conditioned existence — which is like a dream because it lacks any inherent coming or going — is the voidness of that which has neither beginning nor end.

11. *The voidness of that which is not to be discarded*
To discard something means to cast it away or to forsake it, whereas not to discard something means not to give it up. Here it refers to the Mahāyāna: that which is not to be discarded under any circumstances. The voidness that is the very lack of inherent existence of that which is not to be discarded is said to be the

voidness of that which is not to be discarded because such
voidness is its very nature.

12. *The voidness of a phenomenon's own nature*

198   The very essence, i.e. the suchness, of conditioned phenomena is
said to be their very own nature because this very essence of theirs
is not something that has been created by either the shrāvakas, the
199   pratyekabuddhas, the bodhisattvas or the tathāgatas. Its voidness
of inherent existence is thus the voidness of a phenomenon's own
nature.

13. *The voidness of all phenomena*

200   "All phenomena" refers to the eighteen elements, the six contacts,
the six feelings that arise from those contacts and all other material
201   and immaterial, conditioned and unconditioned phenomena. The
voidness that is the absence of inherent existence of all these
phenomena is the voidness of all phenomena.

14. *The voidness of defining characteristics*

The lack of inherent thingness of such defining characteristics as
something's being fit to be form is the voidness of defining characteristics.

202   Form has the defining characteristic of being fit to be form;
feeling has the nature of experiencing; discernment apprehends
the characteristics of things; the formative elements (*'du.byed*)
203   actually constitute conditioned phenomena (*'du.byas*); consciousness has the defining characteristic of cognizing particular objects;
the aggregates have the defining characteristic of unsatisfactori-
ness; and the nature of the elements is likened to that of a
204   poisonous snake. The Buddha taught that the sense-fields
(*skye.mched*) are the very gateways to birth (*skye.ba'i.sgo*). And
whatever arises dependently has the defining characteristics of
being formed and compounded by causes and conditions.
205   The six perfections have the following defining characteristics:
the perfection of generosity is the intention to give away; moral
discipline is a state of being untormented by disturbing con-

ceptions; patience is a state of not being angry; enthusiasm is a state devoid of the unwholesome; absorption gathers the attention to one point; and wisdom is a state of non-attachment. The Omniscient One taught that the defining characteristic of the four absorptions, the four immeasurable states and likewise the four formless states of absorption is that of imperturbability. The thirty-seven facets of enlightenment have the defining characteristic of causing one definitely to go forth to liberation. The first of the three doors to liberation, voidness, has the defining characteristic of absence, because it is not defiled by the stains of the conceptual apprehension of inherent existence. The second door, signlessness, is sheer tranquility; and the defining characteristic of the third door, wishlessness, is the lack of suffering and bewilderment. The defining characteristic of the eight forms of liberation is that of causing total freedom from the obstructions to absorption.

The ten powers of the Buddha have the nature of utter certainty, and the four states of fearlessness that the Lord possesses are of the nature of extreme firmness. His perfect knowledge of individual phenomena, i.e. of dharmas, meanings, words and confident speech, has the defining characteristic of unapproachability. His direct bestowal of benefit to the world is what is known as his great love; his affording complete protection to those who suffer is his great compassion; his great joy is his being supremely joyful; and his great equanimity has the defining characteristic of being unmixed with either attachment or hatred. What are asserted as the eighteen unmixed qualities of the Buddha have the defining characteristic of unassailability, because the Teacher can never be assailed by confusion and so forth. The wisdom of omniscience is regarded as bearing the defining characteristic of being a direct perception of all phenomena. All cognitions other than it are not called direct perceptions of all phenomena because they have only a partial apprehension of their objects.

Thus the voidness of defining characteristics is the voidness of just the inherent existence of the defining characteristics of all conditioned and unconditioned phenomena.

206
207

208

209

210

211

212

213

214

215

15. *The voidness of the non-apprehensible*

216   The three times do not inherently exist because the present does not remain, the past is gone and the future has not yet come. In whichever of these three respects they are not apprehended, in that respect each of the three times is said to be non-apprehensible. Since the non-apprehensible neither remains fixed and static nor perishes, its sheer absence of an inherent nature is the voidness of the non-apprehensible.

217

16. *The voidness of non-things*

218   Because things arise from causes and conditions they lack the nature of being inherently compounded. Therefore they can be called non-things. Thus the voidness of inherent existence of what is compounded is the voidness of non-things.

B. *THE FOUR VOIDNESSES*

1. *The voidness of things*

219   Generally speaking, the term "things" simply denotes the five aggregates. Their voidness of inherent existence is explained as the voidness of things.

2. *The voidness of non-things*

220   In brief, the term "non-things" denotes all unconditioned phenomena. The voidness of inherent existence of those very non-things is said to be the voidness of non-things.

3. *The voidness of nature*

221   The nature of phenomena, i.e. their suchness, is said to be their nature because it is not created by anyone. The lack of an inherent essence in this nature is the voidness of nature.

4. *The voidness that is the other nature*

222   Whether buddhas appear in the world or not, the natural voidness of all things is proclaimed to be their other, i.e. supreme or transcendent, nature. The perfect end, i.e. the nirvana which is the exhaustion of samsara, and suchness are said to constitute the voidness that is the other nature.

223

These different aspects of voidness as they have been explained here were originally proclaimed in the *Perfection of Wisdom Sutras*.

C. CONCLUSION

With rays of wisdom emerging from such analyses the bodhisatt- 224
va on the sixth spiritual level creates a brilliant light that enables him to understand the primordial lack of inherent production of the three realms of existence as clearly as he would see a fresh olive resting in the palm of his hand. Thus in terms of conventional truth he proceeds towards cessation. But although his thought is 225
constantly directed towards cessation, his compassion for the pro- tectorless world continues to develop. Subsequently his mind will come to outshine even the shrāvakas, who are born from the Sugata's speech, as well as all the pratyekabuddhas. This king of 226
swans with his broad white outstretched wings of the paths of con- ventional and ultimate truth soars ahead of the swans of ordinary beings. Through the force of the mighty winds of virtue he flies to the magnificent shores of the ocean of buddha-qualities.

Part Three
Mahāmudrā

Contents of Part Three

Preface to Part Three

The text upon which this presentation of mahāmudrā is based is the *Root Text for the Gelugpa Oral Tradition of Mahāmudrā: The Main Path All Buddhas have Travelled,* composed by the first Panchen Lama, Losang Chökyi Gyaltsen. The origins of this lineage of mahāmudrā are sets of oral instruction received by Tsong Khapa in states of direct spiritual communion with Mañjushri. These teachings on mahāmudrā are essentially practical advice on how to gain a living experience of voidness in meditation. As such, particular emphasis is given to the development of the devotional and meditative framework in which the insight into voidness needs to be nurtured. The presentation of voidness is concise and often cryptic, avoiding any detailed philosophical discussion or argument.

Although mahāmudrā practice is often associated with the tantric aspects of Mahāyāna Buddhism, here Geshé Rabten explains it primarily in terms of the non-tantric, sutra approach. He discusses the various preliminary practices that act as the basis for the meditation as well as the different stages in the meditation itself. Special attention is given to the cultivation of single-pointed mental quiescence focused upon the clear and empty nature of the mind itself. In this state of consciousness one reaches a particularly receptive frame of mind for effectively proceeding to the actual meditation on mahāmudrā.

This explanation was given as a public seminar at Tharpa Choeling, Centre for Higher Tibetan Studies, Switzerland, from the 5th to the 8th of June, 1979.

1 Introduction

We can study dharma for one of two purposes: either to gain certain scholastic knowledge or to derive some real inner benefit. It is true that an intelligent, well-educated person can, by paying careful attention to what he reads, increase his intellectual knowledge of the theories of Buddhism. But this alone is not of much importance; what is really necessary is to elicit from the dharma that which is of practical benefit for our lives. Should we succeed in deriving such benefit, we shall experience a genuine inner contentment which, in turn, will be reflected in our external behaviour towards others. If, however, we fail to develop this inner knowledge and well-being, we shall never succeed in establishing harmonious relationships. Thus, whether we are concerned with our own happiness or others', in either the long or the short term, the essential factor is to discover that which actually benefits and helps our own mind.

The subject matter here is mahāmudrā. What does this term "mahāmudrā" mean? Literally, mahā means great and mudrā means seal. We talk of "sealing a contract." This is done by signing an agreement or, as was done in Tibet, by placing one's personal seal on a document. This act is akin to a promise; it expresses our intention not to stray from our resolve; it signifies that we will not change our mind. Therefore, mudrā should be understood in this sense of inseparability and immutability.

Now, it must be made clear that the term is interpreted differently in the sutra and tantra teachings of the Buddha. First let us consider its meaning according to tantra. By using the special techniques of tantra the meditator is able to arouse an extremely blissful state of consciousness; when such a bliss-consciousness gains an intuitive realization of voidness it is called a seal, or mudrā. The bliss experienced in this state of direct intuition of voidness utterly transcends any kind of pleasure that can be enjoyed through the senses; nothing in the world can compare with it. We should not imagine, however, that anyone who claims to be practising tantra has necessarily achieved this experience. This condition of the great seal, mahāmudrā, occurs only at very advanced stages of the tantric path, and those who have achieved it cannot be separated from it. Whether such a person is meditating, making offerings or simply relaxing, these activities never cease to sustain and stimulate his blissful state of mahāmudrā.

Let us take as an example someone who has a naturally happy disposition. No matter what situation he finds himself in, he is always content. But it is not the situation, be it a landscape or the company of another person, that is the source of his contentment; it is his own subjective disposition. Because of this, everything he encounters assumes an agreeable character. Similarly, but to a much greater degree, everything that a tantric practitioner who has realized mahāmudrā comes into contact with serves to arouse bliss within him. Whatever he sees, hears, tastes, smells or touches always induces a profound delight in his mind. Thus his experience is termed a seal, or mudrā, in the sense of its being always inseparable from delight.

In the sutra tradition, however, mahāmudrā does not signify the subjective experience of voidness but the voidness itself. Voidness means being void of inherent existence and is the ultimate nature of every single phenomenon. There is nothing within the mind, the body or the material world that does not have this fundamental characteristic. It is in this sense of being inseparable from phenomena that voidness is called their seal, or mudrā.

Although the meaning of mahāmudrā is interpreted differently in the tantra and sutra traditions, we should not assume that the voidness they posit is different. It is important to understand that the voidness realized by meditators of both traditions is identical. The difference lies in the quality of the meditator's subjective experience. Thus in the tantra system mahāmudrā refers to the blissful realization of voidness, whereas in the sutra system it refers to voidness itself.

Furthermore, mahāmudrā is the *great* seal. But why is it called great? It is great because, according to the tantric tradition, it is the most powerful inner experience we can develop to destroy the obstructions to liberation and omniscience and, according to the sutra tradition, it is the most important object to realize in order to achieve these goals.

Frequently we find the word "mahāmudrā" on our lips, but rarely do we consider what it really means. The preceding explanation should help to clarify its meaning, specifically in the context of the two traditions of sutra and tantra.

2 The Preliminary Practices

THE GENERAL PRELIMINARIES

The practice of mahāmudrā in the tantric tradition involves very advanced and difficult meditational techniques. Therefore, if we are looking for something we can practise now, we should look to the sutra tradition. In fact it is only on the basis of having gained proficiency in the mahāmudrā meditations as explained in the sutras that we can proceed effectively to the corresponding tantric meditations. We would get nowhere if we were to attempt the tantric practice of mahāmudrā without such a basis.

Before practising mahāmudrā meditation it is essential to prepare ourselves by means of certain preliminaries. A theoretical knowledge of the practice alone is insufficient as a basis for developing actual insights that will have a profound effect on our minds. Suppose that someone has successfully completed his study of architecture. When this person actually wants to build a house according to his preconceived designs, all of his technical expertise will be useless unless he manages to acquire the bricks, beams, cement and other necessities for building. Just as it is essential for such a person to assemble all the necessary conditions for constructing his house, so is it essential for us to establish a firm basis in the preliminary practices before attempting advanced meditations such as mahāmudrā. People frequently complain that, although they have been meditating for a long time, they have not achieved any concrete results: in every case the reason is that they have failed to establish the necessary preparatory basis for their practice. Without such a basis it is certain that the desired results will not be obtained.

But what, exactly, is a preparatory basis? There are two things: the presence of conditions favourable for meditation, i.e. the necessary accumulation of merit, and the absence of conditions unfavourable for meditation, i.e. our various psychological obstacles and hindrances. Let us return to our analogy of the person who wants to build a house. Before he can even start to transport the building materials to the site, he must ensure that it has been cleared of any trees, rocks and other things that could hinder the work. Similarly, first we need to eliminate the negative, obstructive elements from our consciousness and then concentrate on accumulating constructive elements of mind, thus providing a firm basis for our meditation. However, one important difference is, when building a house the clearing of the site must necessarily precede the gathering of building materials there, but in the very act of purifying the mind of obstructive forces we are already accumulating meritorious qualities. In the external example the two processes occur sequentially, whereas in the preparation of the mind for meditation they occur simultaneously.

Five major preliminary practices are taught as the means of preparing the mind for mahāmudrā meditation: the offering of prostrations, recitation of the Vajrasattva mantra, taking refuge in the triple gem, offering the mandala and guru-yoga. The first two (offering of prostrations and recitation of the Vajrasattva mantra) are primarily aimed at purification of mental obstacles, whereas the latter three (taking refuge in the triple gem, offering the mandala and guru-yoga) are primarily concerned with the accumulation of merit. In general one benefits no matter how many of these practices one performs, but there is said to be an especially powerful effect in performing one hundred thousand of each.

Since I have outlined these preliminary practices in detail elsewhere there is no need to give an elaborate explanation of them here.* The following discussion should be seen as additional advice to be understood on the basis of previous acquaintance with the meaning of the preliminary practices.

The offering of prostrations

As the foundation for an effective practice of prostration, it is necessary to have firm confidence in the objects to which we prostrate ourselves: the Buddha, the dharma and the sangha. We should clearly understand what they signify and imagine their presence in the form of a visualization before us. If we repeatedly offer physical prostrations in such a state of mind, positive psychological results will definitely come. But if we fail to cultivate this mental condition, the prostrations will serve merely as a physical exercise and nothing more. Therefore, in order to practise prostration correctly, it is essential that we maintain a constant state of faith and understanding. Should we complete one hundred thousand prostrations in this way, we can be sure that we have achieved genuine and powerful purificatory effects.

However, some people find that even after completing one hundred thousand such prostrations, their minds are still beset with desire and hatred and no results of purification are evident. But the fact that one's manifest state of mind seems unchanged does not necessarily mean that purification has not taken place in the deeper recesses of consciousness. A deep inner cleansing of negative tendencies and obstructions will not always be reflected immediately on the surface of the mind; the reduction of manifest psychological negativities and the purification of unconscious psychological tendencies are related but not necessarily simultaneous phenomena.

In addition, it is helpful to perform the prostrations in conjunc-

* See Geshé Rabten, *The Preliminary Practices*; also *The Life and Teachings of Geshé Rabten*, p. 134 seq.

tion with the application of the four remedial forces: regret for the unwholesome acts one has committed, reliance upon the triple gem, the intention to refrain from unwholesome acts in future, and the intention to cultivate their opposite, i.e. wholesome acts. Moreover, if one can combine the practice with the recitation and contemplation of the *Confession Sutra*, this will be even more beneficial.

The recitation of the Vajrasattva mantra

Recitation of the one-hundred-syllable mantra of Vajrasattva must be combined with the four remedial forces and the appropriate visualizations. Furthermore, it is essential to have firm faith and belief in the ability of this practice to eradicate all negative tendencies of mind. Although the mantra itself has the power (*samaya*, or pledge) to purify negativities and we benefit merely by reciting it, if we do not have strong faith in it, the mantra's positive effect on our mind will be limited. Thus to purify ourselves completely we must have full confidence in the power of the mantra. Once a negative tendency has been imprinted on the mind it does not remain static but, in the absence of counteractive forces, increases in strength day by day. Recitation of the Vajrasattva mantra twenty-one times every night, while not eradicating negativities accumulated during that day, will at least prevent their augmentation. However, recitation of this mantra one hundred thousand times can completely purify previous negativities; even broken tantric vows can be restored through this practice.

How is it that negative tendencies can be eradicated from the mind by offering prostrations and reciting Vajrasattva mantras? First of all let us clarify what is meant by the term "negative tendency" (*sdig.pa*). Every unwholesome act of body, speech or mind leaves an impression in the unconscious that possesses the power to manifest subsequently as an unpleasant experience. Such an impression, or potency, is what is meant here by "negative tendency." These impressions are like seeds. If we plant a barley seed and provide it with the right conditions, it will ripen into a stalk of barley, but if we roast the seed until it turns black its ability to produce its fruit will be destroyed. Similarly, if we just leave negative tendencies in our minds inevitably they will ripen into painful experiences upon meeting the appropriate conditions. But if we make prostrations and recite the Vajrasattva mantra the ability of negativities to bring the fruit of suffering will be destroyed.

Taking refuge in the triple gem

The most important factor in taking refuge is not the verbal recitation of the formula, but our underlying attitude of mind: one of firm belief and confidence in the objects of refuge: the Buddha, the dharma and the sangha. This state of mind is the inner and actual taking of refuge; the words "Namo buddhaya, namo dharmaya, namo sanghaya" are merely the verbal taking of refuge. Reciting the formula without any real conviction will bring no genuinely wholesome results, although it will have the positive effect of at least preventing us from lying, slandering and gossiping while we are reciting. It is only when our verbal recitation is motivated and accompanied by a sincere inner attitude of faith that the taking of refuge becomes fully effective.

If we have not benefited from our past taking of refuge it is because we have not been taking inner refuge, not because of some inherent weakness in the practice itself or an unwillingness of the objects of refuge to help. There must be a state of cooperation between us and the Buddha if our taking refuge is to be effective; if we have no faith in the Buddha he cannot help us. Just as, no matter how hard we try, we cannot clap with one hand alone but must have both hands meet together to produce a sound. Similarly, if we want to take refuge successfully our minds must meet with the Buddha through the agency of faith. Therefore, the taking of refuge does not necessarily entail any verbal incantations. Even when we are lying down and relaxing, if faith in the triple gem is present in our mind, a pure act of taking refuge is occurring and we are Buddhists in the fullest sense of the word.

Offering the mandala

Our usual conception of offering the mandala is that of a rather odd practice in which we twist our fingers into a certain gesture and imagine offering the world complete with continents and mountains to the Buddha. Although we may consider it reasonable to offer our own personal possessions in the form of a mandala, what strikes us as strange is the offering of so many things that we could never hope to own. And even if we could arrange to offer all these things, how could we possibly manage actually to present them to the Buddha? Once again, the problem is that of trying to externalize something that is essentially an inner process.

Offering the mandala is a mental act of giving up, or surrendering, everything. The more things we can conceive of to offer, the more our mind will accumulate wholesome tendencies. The benefit of the practice is dependent upon the vastness of the offering; it does not matter to whom it belongs. However, to make this offering even more meaningful, we should consider that although it appears in the form of all the beautiful and wonderful things in the world, its nature is that of all our wholesome dispositions of the past, present and future.

Still one may object by saying that, although it is possible to offer one's present wholesome dispositions, how can one know that one accumulated any wholesome dispositions in the past? What proof is there that they exist? The proof of their existence is the fact that we are human beings now. The reason we are not experiencing an unfortunate realm of existence but are enjoying a human life is because previously we accumulated the necessary wholesome tendencies to be born as human beings. In the terminology of logic such reasoning is called a "perfect effect indication" (*'bras.rtags.yang.dag*), that is, a case where we are able to infer correctly the presence of a previous cause from a present effect. In this case the effect is a human state of existence from which we are able to infer correctly that a wholesome act necessarily preceded it as its cause. If we recognize human life as an effect, it is a mistake to deny that it had a specific cause, for in nature we are able to see that every effect is invariably the result of its own cause. By means of such reasoning we are able to prove that in the past we must have accumulated wholesome tendencies and dispositions. Therefore, it is fitting to offer them in the form of a mandala now.

We can offer the mandala in four aspects:

The outer mandala. This is composed of all the physical objects of the mandala such as the sun, the moon, Mount Meru, the four continents and so forth.

The inner mandala. This is the offering of all our wholesome dispositions, visualizing the outer mandala as the mere representation of these.

The secret mandala. This is the offering of the blissful nature of the objects, based on the recognition that bliss can arise in dependence upon them.

The ultimate mandala. When we realize that everything we are offering has no inherent existence but exists merely conventionally through the power of imputation, we are offering the ultimate mandala.

To make a genuine offering of the mandala it is not necessary to recite verbally the text of offering or to perform any external actions. If one sincerely makes this offering in the silence of one's contemplation, all the benefits of offering the mandala will ensue.

Guru-yoga

Guru-yoga is an extremely important preliminary that is to be practised not only as a meditation in its own right but also as an integral part of all the other preliminary practices. If, while performing prostrations and the other preliminaries, we make a strong distinction between the teacher who instructs us in these practices and the buddhas and bodhisattvas whom we visualize in the space before us, considering the former as merely an ordinary human being like ourselves and the latter as holy and divine, we are making a great mistake. Although with such an attitude some superficial benefits will result, in essence our practice will be devoid of much meaning.

In every practice and contemplation we do, it is of the utmost importance to realize that the buddhas and bodhisattvas towards whom we direct our attention are in nature inseparable from our own spiritual master, or guru. The only difference between them is in outward appearance; in essence they are identical. It is irrelevant whether our guru is in fact identical in nature with the buddhas or not; the point of the practice is to be convinced from our own side that he is.

In brief, as a practice in itself, guru-yoga should be performed as follows. First visualize your meditational deity, or *yi.dam*, and develop the certainty that in essence this deity is truly your spiritual master. On the basis of this contemplation recite your guru's name-mantra one hundred thousand times. Once again, the most important part of this practice is the strength of your faith.

THE SPECIFIC PRELIMINARIES

An important function of the preliminary practices just explained is to make the mind able to apply itself smoothly and easily to the practice of meditation; they make the mind very supple and flexible. A seed that is planted in fertile soil, is well tended, and receives plenty of water and sunlight, will sprout and grow rapidly with few hindrances. Likewise, mahāmudrā cultivated in the optimum conditions of a mind that has completed these pre-liminaries will develop successfully. But before we can start with the actual explanation of mahāmudrā, there still remain certain other preliminary factors to consider.

First I would like to explain the ideal external conditions for meditation. We should not think, however, that these are absolutely essential for gaining results. They are very helpful if we can find them, but the meditation will still be effective even if we cannot. The surroundings in which we practise meditation should be such that we feel calm and at ease merely by being there.

The place should be quiet and peaceful, the air fresh and clean and the water natural and unpolluted. These conditions will help to keep the body invigorated and healthy, thus making it a good physical basis for spiritual development. Likewise our dwelling place should have a quiet and comfortable feeling about it. Sufficient supplies of food and drink should also be available nearby. In Tibet such conditions were relatively easy to satisfy, but in Western countries today they appear to be increasingly difficult to find.

Another important aid is a friend or helper able to care for our needs and give advice at times of difficulty with the meditation. It is likewise his responsibility to ensure that we are not disturbed by visitors while meditating. Also he should be someone who can give us encouragement and support when we feel depressed and want to stop the practice. If we were left alone there would be the constant danger of our becoming disheartened and, having no one to turn to, ceasing to meditate. It goes without saying that this friend should be someone we get along with very well; any friction in the relationship will only be a hindrance to our meditation. This person should fully agree with whatever we are doing and support us in every respect.

Before embarking on the actual task of meditation we should understand clearly exactly what it entails. We should know of the obstacles that may arise, how to counteract them and how to strengthen and develop the meditation. Without such knowledge, even if we set out to meditate with a strong and sincere desire to develop our minds, we shall make no progress. It is quite meaningless to discard all forms of study, climb to the top of a mountain, sit in a hut and attempt to empty the mind of thought, all in the name of meditation. A blank mind suffering from vague wandering thoughts is of little benefit to anyone. Even someone who aspires to become a doctor, architect or farmer must first complete his studies and training in order to be successful in his chosen career and accomplish his goals. Similarly, if we wish to succeed in this most important of tasks — the taming of the mind and the understanding of reality — it is essential first to gain precise knowledge of how to achieve these goals. Only when we have such knowledge can we feel fully confident and qualified to undertake our task.

In addition to a clear intellectual basis for our meditation, a firm moral basis is necessary. We should not think that moral discipline is something mainly for monks and nuns, and not so important for lay people. Whoever we are, the cultivation of pure morality is indispensable for achieving the goals of meditational practice; without it, insights will never arise. In brief, the foundation of all Buddhist ethical practice is avoidance of the ten unwholesome actions. Even if we cannot strictly refrain from all of them, we should try our best to avoid as many as possible.

Once we have found a suitable place for meditation and are well prepared, we should place ourselves on a seat that is slightly raised at the back and commence the actual session of mahāmudrā meditation. Now, if we try to concentrate immediately on a particular object, or simply start to follow the first thoughts that come to mind, we shall not get very far. The first step of the meditation is to take refuge in the Buddha, dharma and sangha and then to determine the nature of our motivation. We should free our minds of all selfish motivation — the negative desire for fame or happiness in this life — and generate instead the highest motivation — a purely altruistic desire to attain enlightenment for the welfare of all others.

At this point, in order to prepare our mind further for the principal meditation, we can perform the six preliminary practices in conjunction with recitation of the *Lam Rim Puja*. Alternatively we can recite the *Hundreds of Deities of the Land of Joy*, a guru-yoga prayer directed towards Tsong Khapa, or the *Inseparability of the Spiritual Master with Avalokiteshvara*, a similar prayer concentrating on the deity Avalokiteshvara. No matter which text we choose, the important thing is to contemplate and say the prayer sincerely from the heart.

It is also important to precede the meditation with some form of breathing exercise. We can either simply concentrate for a while on the inflow and outflow of the breath or perform the nine-round breathing meditation. In the latter, each round comprises an inhalation and its accompanying exhalation. In the first three rounds we inhale through the right nostril and exhale through the left; in the next three we inhale through the left and exhale through the right; and in the last three rounds we inhale and exhale through both nostrils together. We can combine this breathing meditation with visualization of the three major energy channels in the body, imagining the breath to be purifying the channels. This makes the practice more powerful than one done without visualization, but the visualization is not essential.*

In addition, the contemplation of "taking and giving" can be incorporated with this breathing practice: as we inhale we visualize that all the suffering, obstacles and negative tendencies of all sentient beings enter our body in the form of black smoke and descend to our heart centre, where they destroy all traces of our self-cherishing. As we exhale we visualize that all our positive qualities leave our body in the form of white light and go to all sentient beings, eliminating all their sufferings and bringing them all happiness. By adding this contemplation we transform the breathing exercise into a Mahāyanā practice through which an awakening mind can be cultivated. In this way we accumulate a much stronger force of merit.

We should not be anxious that these preliminaries are taking up all the time we had set aside for meditating on mahāmudrā and perform them hastily with little interest. They must be done in a relaxed and calm manner. It is quite permissible to shorten them if we do not have much time, but under no circumstances should they be rushed. The function of these preliminaries is twofold: to accumulate wholesome tendencies in the mind and to provide a basis of purity and calm for effectively engaging in the principal meditation. As long as we keep stirring and shaking a bucket of water, the water will remain turbulent and agitated; but if we set it down and it remains unmoved, the turbulence will slowly cease and the water will become calm and clear. Similarly, if all the turmoil, worry and agitation in the mind are gradually pacified and brought to rest by the preliminaries, we can achieve the necessary

---

* See McDonald, Kathleen, *Basic Buddhist Meditations*, for descriptions of breathing meditations and the psychic channels.

peace and clarity of mind to be able to continue successfully with the main meditation.

As a final step before commencing the principal meditation we should visualize in the space before us our spiritual master, having the firm conviction that he embodies the very essence of the wisdom, compassion, power and blessings of all the buddhas. As mentioned before, it is of the utmost importance never to consider our spiritual master, or guru, as being in any way distinct from a buddha. Although they may be different in name, in essence they are identical. When this fact is borne in mind, whatever contemplation or meditation we perform will be far more powerful and effective.

We should now direct our entire attention to our spiritual master with as much faith and devotion as we can muster. The recollection of his kindness and excellent qualities should generate such faith that we are moved to tears and even the hairs on our body stand on end. Ideally it is devotion such as this that should be generated prior to the meditation. While visualizing the spiritual master in this way, we should make requests and offerings to him as described in the various texts on guru-yoga. Next we should concentrate on reciting his name-mantra, praying all the time that he might impart his blessings so that our meditation on mahāmudrā will be fruitful. Simultaneously with the recitation of the mantra we can imagine many streams of light and nectar issuing from his radiant body and penetrating our own, purifying us of all obstacles and negative tendencies.

Next we should visualize the spiritual master dissolving, through the force of our faith and devotion and his being extremely pleased with our prayers and requests, into white or yellow light, which enters our body through the crown of the head, descends to the region of the heart-centre and merges inseparably with our own mind. As a result, we immediately experience such great bliss that our mind comes completely to rest within its sphere and thoughts of all other objects cease. This bliss is beyond compare with any ordinary, worldly sense experience. Moreover, it will arise only when the preceding factors of faith and devotion have been genuinely developed through contemplation of the guru's qualities. Once it has occurred we should try to dwell single-pointedly within its sphere for as long as possible, not allowing any mundane memories, thoughts or expectations to arise.

Normally we find ourselves preoccupied with superficial difficulties and problems. But however much we fret and worry about them they will not stop — even at death. If, however, we concentrate on meditations such as this, these trifling problems will cease to torment us and our lives will become far more meaningful. My intention in describing this contemplation of the guru has not been simply to glorify spiritual teachers but to show the degree of faith we should have in the teacher prior to engaging in the principal mahāmudrā meditation.

3 The Principal Meditation

MENTAL QUIESCENCE

To practise the principal meditation on mahāmudrā we have to develop two things: meditation and view. Here, meditation refers to attaining mental quiescence and view to gaining a precise understanding of voidness. Generally, there are two means of cultivating them. In the first we start by making an intellectual analysis of the nature of voidness; when we have gained an understanding of it we develop mental quiescence; finally we concentrate our mind upon voidness as we have understood it. This method is called "developing meditation on the basis of the view." The second way of realizing mahāmudrā is called "developing the view on the basis of meditation." Here we first cultivate mental quiescence, and only when we have attained it do we start to analyze voidness. Whether we follow one approach or the other depends largely upon our personal disposition. Some people are more inclined to begin with study and intellectual analysis; others prefer to start immediately with the practice of mental quiescence. The final result of these two approaches is the same; it is only the sequence that differs. In either case, however, it is important for the preliminary practices explained above to precede our analytical or concentrative meditations.

There is, however, an advantage to the second method. Imagine a painting on a wall illuminated by candle. If a window is open the candle will flicker, making it difficult to distinguish the features of the painting, but if the window is closed the flame will remain steady, enabling us to see every detail clearly. Similarly, if we try to analyze voidness with a mind that has not achieved mental quiescence, it will be difficult to keep our concentration on the object for any sustained period of time since our mind will flicker like a candle. If, however, we have realized mental quiescence, our mind will be perfectly steady and able to concentrate on the object of meditation without any risk or distraction. In such a state it is considerably easier to analyze and thereby determine the nature of voidness. Thus the method I shall now explain will be the second one: developing the view on the basis of meditation.

There are many ways in which mental quiescence can be developed. Usually it is explained that one should visualize a particular object, such as the form of a buddha or a drop of light, and concentrate the mind single-pointedly upon it. But here a special means will be taught: the attainment of mental quiescence through concentrating on the clear and empty nature of the mind itself. This has the particular advantage of enabling us to make a relatively easy transition to the meditation on voidness, the object in each case being similar: devoid of any material content such as shape or colour. Hence first we learn to concentrate on the clear and empty nature of the mind and then proceed to transfer our concentration to voidness: the emptiness of inherent existence. If, on the other hand, we use the visualized form of a buddha to develop mental quiescence, a conventional fabrication that appears to us vividly in shape and colour remains present in our mind and to shift our concentration to a non-material, abstract entity such as voidness becomes that much more difficult.

Although the development of mental quiescence through concentration on the mind itself has this great advantage, there are also certain disadvantages and dangers involved. The first disadvantage is the difficulty of locating the object upon which we are to concentrate. When meditating upon the form of a buddha, for example, the questions of what the object of meditation is like or where it is do not arise. But since the mind itself is devoid of any colour or shape, when we try to find out what it is like and where it is, we encounter many difficulties. In practice, it is extremely hard to identify and locate the mind as an object of concentration.

The second disadvantage is the danger of developing nervous tension and strain. If we focus our concentration inwards upon the mind itself, we run the risk of upsetting the energy-winds in the body and causing nervous disorders which, if prolonged, can lead to breakdowns. When the mind is concentrated outwards to a visualized object, however, this danger is greatly reduced. Therefore, we must be careful in attempting to develop mental quiescence using the mind as the object. If we find that it requires too much strain and causes agitation and unrest, we should try to concentrate upon an externally visualized object instead.

I have already pointed out the difficulty involved in actually identifying and locating the mind. Therefore, before we can proceed to focus our concentration upon it, it is necessary to make some observations about the nature of the mind in order to help us recognize it. Trying to meditate on the mind without first having some idea of what it is is like groping around in the dark.

Each of us is conscious of the fact that we have a mind, but few of us have a clear idea of exactly what the mind is. What is the nature of the mind? Our immediate reply may be that it is the knowing faculty of the person: that which perceives and thinks. But such a conception fails to answer the question adequately. The characteristics we have just mentioned are indeed evident to us but simply to recognize them in such a manner does not enable us to grasp the essence of mind.

Let us consider the matter more carefully. One defining characteristic of the mind is its quality of being devoid of physical properties: it has no colour, no shape and it cannot be touched. But its essence is not merely this lack of material content; space too is clear and empty in this way, but it is not mind. The difference between the mind and space is that the former is a dynamic, temporal phenomenon that undergoes momentary change, whereas space is non-temporal and not subject to such change. The mind is always arising in dependence upon its preceding causes and conditions, which include both other states of mind and material phenomena. In addition to being clear and empty of any physical properties, it is in a constant state of trans-formation. Furthermore, this dynamic property of mind has the quality of cognition. Cognition is a defining characteristic of the mind which indicates that every one of its particular instances and states necessarily apprehends a specific object. This is something we can investigate for ourselves; we can see how every thought is a thought *of* something and every perception is a perception *of* a particular object.

Moreover, the mind is very powerful; it is the overlord of body and speech. All the physical and vocal actions we engage in are in-variably directed by the mind. Mind is also the determining factor of experience. If we acquaint it with a wholesome course of be-haviour, it will increase well-being and understanding and finally will even reach the state of buddha consciousness. But if it falls into mistaken and unwholesome modes of cognition and conduct, it will experience unfortunate and unhappy conditions of exis-tence.

It is, indeed, possible to give a more detailed account of the primary and secondary aspects of mind, their functions, relations and so forth, but for the development of mental quiescence a des-cription of the mind's essential nature alone is sufficient. It must be stressed, however, that before we can begin developing concen-tration on the mind, we must have gained an apprehension of its basic characteristics. This requires a process of analysis in which we repeatedly examine and reflect upon the mind with a view to recognizing and thus ascertaining its fundamental properties of clarity, emptiness and cognition. If we persevere with such an analysis, these characteristics will become more and more apparent, until finally they become quite clear and evident to us. It does not matter how long it takes us to gain this recognition, we must continue to try, for without it the meditation cannot begin. Once we have achieved a clear recognition of the mind in this way, the next step is to focus carefully upon the nature of the mind. First of all we should not allow any thoughts to dwell on the past or to stray into the future. Our awareness should remain solely in the present. In other forms of contemplation it is often very beneficial to reflect on the future stages of the path, the benefits of developing and purifying the mind and so forth; this helps to strengthen our motivation and gives us a sense of purpose. But here the meditation requires that the mind be concentrated only on the present moment, upon the mind as it is now.

The process of developing mental quiescence on the mind requires nothing but the constant and mindful application of recollection upon the object of meditation. It is simply a question of recognizing the mind and remaining aware of it. Once our recollection has focused upon the mind, we should try never to let it out of our sight. Imagine playing with a young puppy by dangling a piece of string in front of its nose only to snatch it away before it can seize it with its teeth. But once the puppy manages to get hold of the string, it will never let go; wherever we pull the string the puppy follows. Similarly, once we have focused our attention upon the clear and empty nature of the mind, we should never let it slip away from us.

At the beginning of the meditation session we find that our recollection of the object is forceful and alert and we have little difficulty in maintaining awareness of the mind. As the session continues, however, the recollection tends to lose strength and the ability to concentrate. This weakening is evidenced by the gradual re-emergence of uncontrolled wandering thoughts in the mind. But wandering thoughts do not necessarily indicate only a decline in mindfulness; they can also indicate that the object itself has been lost. As the recollection of the clear and empty nature of the mind declines, our awareness may degenerate into an awareness of mere vacuity. We lose the recollection of the mind and instead find ourselves concentrating on a mere absence of all content. As soon as we notice this, it is necessary immediately to resume the meditation from the beginning. Once again we should recognize the nature of the mind and carefully proceed to remain mindful of it. One helpful technique for regaining our awareness is to wait for a feeling of pleasure or pain to manifest in the mind. Such feelings are immediately noticeable and it is relatively easy to recognize their clear and empty nature and thus resume the meditation.

Usually we speak of two mental factors as being instrumental in the development of mental quiescence: recollection, which we have already mentioned, and alertness. However, in the beginning stages of this meditation, it is recollection that needs to be especially cultivated. As we begin the practice of mental quiescence we shall find that our recollection of the object cannot sustain itself for long and is frequently interrupted by other thoughts. But as we continue in the meditation, the strength and duration of our recollection will gradually increase. At the outset there may be times when the mind seems constantly beset with the surgings of uncontrolled thoughts and meditation seems nearly impossible. Relentless perseverence and regular practice are the only antidotes here, however difficult it may seem. If we apply ourselves sincerely to the meditation and follow the instructions we are given, the hindrances will decrease and the mind will reach distinct levels of stability.

In all there are nine levels of stability through which we need to pass before achieving mental quiescence.* During the first two levels the mind achieves a certain ability to remain single-pointedly upon the object but is still frequently overwhelmed by the force of wandering thoughts and loses the object altogether. It is only on the third level that the mind gains sufficient stability to be able to regain its hold quickly on the object after being upset by distracting thoughts. At this level we also gain the ability to detect wandering thoughts the moment they arise and thereby cut them off before they can disturb our concentration.

What happens in the mind of a meditator at this level is similar to what happens in a boxing match between two competitors of equal skill and strength; here the force of recollection and the force of uncontrolled thoughts are equal in strength. Occasionally we prevent the wandering thoughts from disturbing us and occasionally they manage to distract us from our object of medit-

* See Geshé Rabten, *The Life and Teachings of Geshé Rabten*, p.165

ation. As we persevere, however, we shall reach the fourth level of stability, where wandering thoughts still occur but are no longer able to distract our mind; no matter what thoughts arise, we never lose our recollection of the clear and empty nature of the mind. Now our mind can be compared to a lake that remains calm in spite of the movement of many fish beneath its surface. Various thoughts may come and go but they are incapable of affecting the general tranquility of consciousness.

Often, when we see someone sitting quietly in meditation, we assume that his mind is likewise calm and peaceful. In fact, if he is sincerely involved in combating the disturbing and distorted elements of his mind, there could be a great amount of activity and turmoil occurring. This is the process that has to take place in meditation. We are quite mistaken if we consider meditation involves only sitting still and lazily doing nothing. If this were the case we might as well just sleep. It is true that these meditational exercises can produce nervous tension and strain, but we should be content that, for once, our nerves have been upset through engaging in something worthwhile.

There are two specific obstacles to the development of mental quiescence: excitement and sinking. They must not be confused with distraction and dullness. When trying to concentrate, frequently we find ourselves distracted and agitated, but such distraction is not necessarily what we mean by excitement here. Excitement is a specific form of distraction that leads the mind away from the object of meditation with thoughts of desirable and attractive things. When the mind is distracted by objects other than these we say general wandering or distraction is present, not excitement. In order to counteract excitement, once we have identified it, it is helpful to contemplate the negative and painful character of existence; conversely, when the mind is depressed, we should reflect on the positive, joyful aspects of life. By following such contemplations, we shall regain our mental equilibrium and be able to pursue the practice of mental quiescence free from these obstacles.

A similar distinction needs to be made between sinking and dullness. Most types of lethargy and cloudiness we experience at the beginning of our meditation practice are merely dullness, which is a mental factor that dulls our awareness and leads us to drowsiness and sleep. Sinking is a more subtle form of dullness that we encounter only when we have achieved the stability of a firm and sustained recollection of the object characterized by suppleness and a joyous feeling; we experience its subtlest form only when we have reached the fourth and fifth levels of stability. Sinking is a decrease in the strength of concentration where our attentive recollection and force of apprehension of the meditation object gradually decrease. However, since recollection and the mind's hold on the object are merely weakened, not completely lost, and the mind is still accompanied by joy, we might mistake sinking for a higher level of stability. Many meditators have been deceived by the most subtle form of sinking, believing it to be mental quiescence itself, and have dwelt in it for long periods of time without realizing that their minds were becoming progressively duller instead of sharper. The end result of this process is a weakening of the force of recollection such that the object is lost altogether. However, although it is important to be aware of the dangers of sinking, we do not have to worry about them too much at present; we have enough work to do combating distraction, excitement and dullness.

Doubts and questions may also cause us much difficulty at the beginning of our practice. Unless they are resolved and answered before we set out to develop mental quiescence they may cause a great deal of distraction. If our meditation is not going well we might start doubting its value; many questions that we cannot answer may arise. Thus, as I have already mentioned, before starting to practise meditation seriously we must understand clearly what it necessitates, where it leads and what are its benefits. Such understanding not only saves us from distracting doubts and questions but gives us a firm intellectual foundation and the necessary confidence for successful pursuit of the goals of meditation.

If you know anything about cattle you will know how unwise it is to tether a young calf in the middle of a field. Instead of calmly eating grass, a calf tied like this will continually strain at the rope, trying to get free. However, an untied calf does not wander far, it simply grazes quietly within self-imposed limits. Similarly, a mind tied by the rope of unresolved doubts and unanswered questions is beset by tension and conflict and constantly strains to be rid of them. Once free, the mind stops trying to wander and comes to rest in an open space where meditation can be practised successfully. In worldly matters our experience teaches us that a strong sense of purpose and direction helps us achieve our goals; this is equally true for the practice of meditation.

Often we think that meditation is an arduous task requiring much effort and determination. We force our body into an uncomfortable posture and over-exert ourselves in our attempts to concentre the mind. Such an attitude causes us to become very tense and rigid and the end result is the exact opposite of the peace of mind we set out to achieve. It is important, therefore, that the body and mind be relaxed and at ease when we meditate. But this relaxed attitude must not degenerate into sloppiness and laziness; we should be free from tension but at the same time remain alert and attentive. Perhaps you have had the experience of removing lice from your hair. If so, you will know that there is a way of holding the louse between your fingers so that the little creature is neither squeezed to death nor allowed to escape back into your hair. The louse must be held both gently and firmly. Similarly, in meditation the mind needs to be in a state that is neither too tense nor too relaxed. A middle way of gentle firmness has to be achieved.

There is an interesting story in one of the sutras that provides a clear illustration of how alert and mindful we should be while developing mental quiescence. The Buddha recounts how a competition was once held between the most skilful swordsman and the most skilful archer in the land. During the match the archer was required to fire as many arrows as he could at the swordsman who in turn was required to deflect each arrow with his sword before it struck him. For a while the swordsman had no difficulty in warding off the arrows; his alertness was such that he succeeded in intercepting the arrows no matter how rapidly they were fired at him. All was going well until, for a fraction of a second, the swordsman's attention was distracted by an attractive woman in the crowd. This momentary loss of alertness cost him his life, for during that second he failed to notice an arrow, which evaded his sword and pierced his heart.

Similarly, a meditator should imagine himself to be a skilful swordsman, realizing that if he lets his mind wander for a moment, it might mean his downfall. The arrows being constantly fired at us during meditation are those of distracted and excited thoughts. Ideally we should be mindful of them as soon as they arise and then cut them off before they have the chance to disturb us. As soon as such a thought manages to escape our attention it will destroy our concentration in the same way as the unnoticed arrow was able to kill the swordsman. The main point here is that when our recollection of the object is firm and unwavering there will be no danger of its being agitated by wandering thoughts, but if we lose our recollection for even a moment, a wandering thought may easily destroy our concentration.

However, for beginners it may prove rather frustrating to model ourselves on the swordsman in our story. If we have not achieved a steady and sustained recollection of the object, it will be very difficult to observe each wandering thought as it arises and immediately eliminate it. In fact, to attempt this now could create more problems than it solves. By trying too hard to control the arisal of thoughts in the mind we may find that they increase rather than decrease. Over-exertion in a technique that is beyond our capacity will usually give rise to much agitation and nervous strain.

For most of us, at present it would be more advisable to adopt the following method of dealing with wandering thoughts. Instead of attempting to cut off each thought as soon as it occurs we should simply stand back and carefully observe the process taking place. Watch the thoughts arise, follow them as they wander about and finally observe them disappear, all the time retaining an attentive stance of objectivity. Observing our thoughts in this way, without reacting to or identifying with them, will cause them to vanish automatically and return to the sphere of clear and empty cognition from which they arose. In ancient times when ships set out on long ocean voyages the sailors would often keep a caged bird on board, to help them know when they were approaching land. They would release the bird, let it fly away and follow its course. If they were still a long way from land, the bird would circle around the ship in all directions and finally return. Likewise we should watch the course of wandering thoughts that arise during our meditation. Just like a bird released from a ship in mid-ocean, they will have no alternative but to return to their starting point.

We should select a method for eliminating wandering thoughts that suits us best. We should not try to put all the methods into practice at once — first trying one, then another and then yet another. Instead, we should first choose one method and concentrate on developing it until we become skilled at applying it. Then, as soon as our mind has been cleared of distracted thoughts and so forth, we should seize the opportunity to recognize the clear and empty nature of the mind and focus our entire recollection upon it. It would be most unwise, having made so much effort to dispel unwanted thoughts, to idly enjoy this temporary state of mental peace. When we are walking on a high mountain on a cloudy day we take advantage of every break in the clouds to appreciate the beautiful view below. It would be foolish, having waited for the clouds to part, to lie down on the mountain-side and go to sleep. Similarly, it is important to persevere with cultivating mental quiescence as soon as the obscuring distracted thoughts disperse.

The manner of focusing recollection upon the object is explained traditionally by six analogies.

Like the sun shining in a cloudless sky. This is analogous to a state of meditation in which all wandering thoughts, distractions, dullness and doubts have been dispelled and the clear and empty nature of the mind appears vividly to our recollection. In such a state there is nothing hindering us from discerning the object precisely and maintaining awareness of it. It must be pointed out, however, that such a state of awareness is only conscious of the *conventional* nature of the mind, i.e. its quality of being clear and cognitive. The realization of the mind's ultimate nature, its voidness of inherent existence, is something quite different. The sole aim of this meditation is to achieve single-pointed concentration on this conventional nature.

Like an eagle soaring through the sky. When an eagle flies it does not flap its wings all the time but glides gracefully, beating its wings only occasionally to add impetus to its flight. Ideally, our meditation should proceed in a similar fashion. For most of the time we should remain steadily absorbed in the object of our concentration, like the gliding eagle. When the occasional wandering thought arises we should dispel it with one or two strokes of analytical contemplation, in the same way the eagle calmly yet forcefully beats its wings, and return to our meditation. At the beginning of our practice it is, of course, necessary to give more attention to cultivation of the analytical faculty to be able to cognize the object of meditation and effectively remove the obstacles to concentration. But at this stage of meditation it is not so important to maintain such a strong sense of analysis. Concerning ourselves too much with looking for wandering thoughts when our concentration is already well developed may actually hinder the meditation instead of helping it. A skilful meditator is one who knows exactly how much analysis to apply and when to apply it. He applies neither too little when much is required nor too much when only a little is needed. Someone who is aware of these points can only progress in his development of mental quiescence. It needs to be borne in mind, however, that these analogies are pertinent only to concentrative meditation; we should not regard them as a description of analytical and contemplative meditation.

Like an ocean. Although its surface may be ruffled by waves, the ocean itself cannot be shaken or moved. During meditation our mind should be like an ocean. Even if it is superficially agitated by a few wandering thoughts, its depths should remain calm and undisturbed. Whatever thoughts occur on the periphery should not distract the mind from the calm recollection of its clear and empty nature.

Like a small child looking at a painting. When a young child stands in front of a painting he does not look at it critically, examining the details. He simply stares at it in its entirety with an open and non-analytical mind. Likewise, when concentrating on the object of meditation, we should not apprehend it in a critical or analytical fashion, always inquiring into its nature, characteristics, functions and so forth, but instead simply focus the mind on the bare presence of the object and let it dwell there in single-pointed concentration.

Like the tracks of a bird in the sky. When we watch a bird flying we can follow its course, but once it has passed we are unable to see any traces of the flight remaining in the sky. Usually the experience of a pleasurable feeling during meditation is followed by attachment and craving for it; when a painful feeling occurs we crave to get rid of it; when neither occurs we remain uninterested and confused. In this way we can say that our feelings leave traces or tracks in the mind: the various reactions they produce. Ideally we should observe the arising and passing away of these feelings as though they were birds flying through the sky. They should come into view, remain for a while and disappear without leaving any trace of their presence in the form of agitated reactions such as attachment, aversion and confusion.

Like dandelion seeds. When the wind blows, dandelion seeds are immediately borne into the air because they are so light in weight. In our meditation the body and mind should also feel very light and buoyant. Frequently the opposite is true. The body feels heavy, unmanageable and uncomfortable, and the mind seems to be dull and lethargic. In such a state it is difficult to make any progress at all. The meditation can only proceed well when not only the mind is light, clear and flexible, but the body too feels buoyant and even weightless. At such times we feel that we could physically rise into the air and float away.

Once mental quiescence has been attained, the meditator will have the ability to remain effortlessly concentrated upon any object he cares to choose. In addition to this tremendous single-pointedness of mind he will also achieve an extremely heightened clarity of awareness, such that when he looks at a rock or a wall, even the tiniest particles will be evident. The body too is experienced as very light and buoyant and it develops a pure and radiant complexion. The reason for this is that at this stage we no longer need to subsist on gross food but are physically sustained by the "food" of concentration. In other words, we derive the necessary nourishment for the body from our state of mental quiescence. It is because we have to rely on gross foods at present that our body usually feels so heavy and cumbersome.

In this description of the various means for developing mental quiescence, the meditation may have appeared to us as a very arduous process involving the removal of all kinds of obstacles and the development of seemingly impossible degrees of awareness. But for someone who has accomplished mental quiescence there is absolutely no difficulty or effort in remaining concentrated on the object because his mind merges inseparably with its clear and empty nature, upon which he has focused his recollection. Now, it is easy to mistake such an absorption for the realization of voidness. They both have many characteristics in common, such as the merging of the mind with the object of meditation and an experience of "emptiness." But in fact this state of absorption is only a preliminary step towards the actual realization of mahāmudrā or voidness. It is only an experience of the conventional nature of the mind and not a realization of its ultimate truth.

As we arise from single-pointed mental quiescence on the nature of the mind and become conscious of the world about us, we may again be deceived into thinking we have achieved a realization of voidness. Before we attain such mental quiescence the external world appears to be composed of objects that seem very stable, concrete and objectively existent, but after we have been absorbed in the clear and empty nature of the mind, the world appears to be quite insubstantial. Physical objects appear as though they were mere reflections in a clear mirror and their concreteness seems no more substantial than that of a rainbow. This experience may lead us to the conclusion that we are experiencing the illusion-like quality of all phenomena, the realization of which is frequently mentioned as a result of having understood voidness. Once again we would have confused two similar but essentially different experiences. The reason we behold things as insubstantial upon rising from this meditation is because we have just been absorbed for a long time in concentrating on the empty and insubstantial nature of the mind. The sense of insubstantiality has been so ingrained in our consciousness that when we look at the world around us, it too appears insubstantial and mirage-like. This experience is a residual after-effect of our meditative concentration. It is somewhat similar to what happens when we have been looking at a bright patch of light and then turn our eyes away and look elsewhere. Our vision is still affected by the image of the patch of light and it is not until several minutes have passed that we can free ourselves of this after-image and see things normally.

Although such experiences carry the danger of our confusing them with the realization of voidness, it is precisely because of them that the development of mental quiescence on the clear and empty nature of the mind is such an excellent basis for the meditation on mahāmudrā. By learning to concentrate on the nature of the mind we develop the ability to concentrate on a phenomenon that is partly characterized by a negation: the negation of material content. This then greatly assists us in shifting our concentration to voidness, since voidness too is characterized by a negation: the negation of inherent existence. Because of this similarity between the two objects we are able to proceed smoothly into the actual meditation on mahāmudrā. Not only are the experiences gained in formal concentration similar, but the post-meditational experiences also resemble each other closely. In both cases phenomena appear to be insubstantial and illusory. Thus, in this respect too we find ourselves in a good position to pursue the realization of voidness.

In brief, the benefits of developing mental quiescence on the clear and empty nature of the mind are threefold: we gain an understanding of the nature of the mind; we achieve a powerful state of concentration that we can direct to whatever object we choose; and we attain the best possible basis upon which to develop the understanding of voidness. It should also be pointed out that the manner of concentrating the mind on voidness is the same as that of concentrating it on the nature of the mind; the only difference is the object.

MAHĀMUDRĀ

As we have mentioned already, in the sutra tradition "mahā-mudrā" means voidness. Now, it is only through the under-standing of voidness that liberation from cyclic existence is possible. As long as we fail to realize it, the cycle of birth and death, pain and frustration will continue uninterrupted. Insight into voidness is therefore called "the gateway to liberation." To understand it is the way to attain the qualities of all the arhats and buddhas; to remain ignorant of it is the cause for all bondage and suffering.

The sutras or discourses delivered by Buddha on voidness are known as the essential sutras. Although the Buddha taught on a wide range of topics, including impermanence, loving kindness, compassion and the awakening mind, his aim was always to lead his disciples to the understanding of voidness. In Shāntideva's *Guide to the Bodhisattva's Way of Life* there is a well known line (IX: 1): "All of these practices were taught by the Mighty One for the sake of wisdom." The practices referred to here are the per-fections of giving, morality, patience, enthusiasm and con-centration as well as the understanding of the four noble truths and so forth. These, says Shāntideva, were taught expressly so that we could cultivate the wisdom that realizes voidness.

But what, we may well ask, do the practices of giving and morality, for example, have to do with the understanding of voidness? How can they possibly lead us to such a realization? By putting into practice the teachings of the awakening mind, the perfections and the four noble truths, we accumulate a powerful store of wholesome tendencies that act as the necessary basis upon which voidness is realized. Voidness does not just appear to us out of the blue. Insight into it can be gained only when a firm spiritual foundation has been laid. Therefore, the Buddha also stated that only those with sufficient merits are capable of approaching voidness.

A particular benefit of contemplating the meaning of the laws of cause and effect and dependent arising prior to engaging in meditation on voidness is that it prevents us from falling into the extreme of nihilism. If we have no understanding of these points and proceed directly to an investigation of voidness, we may draw the false conclusion that since all things are void they do not exist. Thus, we may entertain the nihilist standpoint, which has extremely counterproductive intellectual and moral consequences. Although for most of us there may not be too great a danger of succumbing to nihilism, it is nevertheless worthwhile to point out the possible wrong paths we may find ourselves following in our attempt to understand voidness. If we are not conscious of them, we may easily deceive ourselves into thinking that we are meditating on voidness when, in fact, the mind is just vaguely concentrating on a mere absence of content. To make a study of these possible pitfalls can, in the long run, save us a lot of wasted time and energy. I must repeat that before we can successfully engage in any form of meditation, we must gain a clear understanding of exactly what the meditation necessitates. To make such an extensive preliminary inquiry is the first stage in opening the eye of wisdom. Only when we see precisely what lies before us can we effectively put it into practice in meditation.

In speaking of voidness we are speaking of the voidness of *something*. Therefore, to understand voidness in relation to a particular object—for example, one's own self— it is necessary to understand what the self is void of. The voidness of the self is its voidness of inherent existence. Thus the realization of voidness requires a process of negation whereby we gain the insight that something we previously assumed to exist—the self's inherent existence—is in fact non-existent. It would be quite absurd to attempt to meditate on voidness without first recognizing exactly what is to be negated. It would be like an archer trying to score a bull's-eye without having located the target; or like a policeman trying to arrest a thief in a crowd without first having identified the thief: he will either arrest the wrong person, fail to arrest anyone, search for the thief elsewhere or be forced to detain the whole crowd.

Nowadays there are many misconceptions about the nature of

voidness. Some people think that meditation on voidness means simply emptying the mind of all content and calmly resting in this mental vacuity. But this is merely a blank state of mind; it has nothing whatsoever to do with voidness. Another misconception is that voidness means the lack of a self or an I. This leads people to think that if they could attain a state of consciousness in which no thought of I arose, they would realize voidness. But it is not as simple as this. We have to discriminate between the self that is falsely imagined and is to be negated, and the self that does exist.

To be more precise, we can distinguish three distinct conceptions of the self. The first is the conception of a self that we have realized to be void of any inherent existence and that we understand to exist conventionally as a mere imputation; the second is that of a self we apprehend as inherently existent; the third is that of a self we consider neither as inherently existent nor as not inherently existent. This third self is the self or I that goes to work, eats dinner and reads these words. Of these three, the first can be clearly perceived only after one has realized voidness; the second is what we call "self-clinging" and the third is the non-reflective, everyday sense of I. The first and the third conceptions of the self are valid and their corresponding referents are existent; they are not to be negated. It is only the second conception that is false, and in this meditation we shall be solely concerned with negating the self that it conceives as its referent.

Now let us return to the actual practice of meditation. I shall assume that we have achieved mental quiescence and have eliminated all wandering thoughts, excitement and sinking, and are now dwelling single-pointedly on the clear and empty nature of the mind. The only thing appearing to us is this clear, empty cognition; no forms or fabrications are present. The next step is to extract carefully one small section of the mind from this concentration and start to employ it in an analytical capacity. It is very difficult to awaken the analytical faculty without disturbing the poise of the concentration. We may find that when we are concentrating we are unable to analyze and when we are analyzing we cannot concentrate. The two functions seem to hinder one another. It requires much practice to be able to perform both simultaneously. But although this may be the case now, when we have actually achieved complete mental quiescence it will not be difficult to analyze and concentrate at the same time.

The first object towards which we should turn our analysis is the meditator himself. When we have attained mental quiescence we shall be able to make this analysis without ever being distracted by any uncontrolled thoughts. These conditions enable the analysis to be particularly penetrating. When a thief finds himself in an unlit bank vault on a dark night, he is able to go about his business without any worries of being interrupted or hindered. Similarly, in a state of total mental quiescence, the analytical aspect of the mind is free to perform whatever investigation it wishes. Let us call this particular meditator "John." Upon thorough analysis it will be discovered that John does not inherently exist within the body and mind, but is merely conceptually imputed upon them. It is up to each of us to determine this mode of existence of our own I.

We say that the I or the self is "merely nominal" or "merely imputed." But what does it mean to be merely imputed? Imagine that you are looking from a distance at a coil of striped rope. You might easily mistake it for a snake and approach it cautiously, convinced that it is a real living snake. But as you get closer you come to realize that it is not a snake at all, merely a coil of rope. The snake in this example was merely an imputation of the mind. Similarly, we may look at a pile of rocks on a hilltop and mistake it for a person. We think to ourselves, "Look, there's someone over there." But as we go closer to see who it is, we realize that no one is there; only a pile of rocks is present. Once again, the person we saw was merely imputed upon the pile of rocks by our mind. In describing this mental function as "imputation" we should not be misled into thinking that it is a particularly mysterious quality of consciousness. It simply refers to the mind's *apprehension* of the object. To state that a snake is imputed to the rope is equivalent to saying that the rope is apprehended as a snake.

Likewise, when we analyze the meditator, we shall arrive at the conclusion that there is no meditator, no I or self, other than the I that is merely apprehended by the mind, that is to say, conceptually imputed by the mind. There is no self that has an inherent, substantial and concrete existence independent of conceptual imputation. There is no meditator John who can, as it were, suddenly appear from his own side and proclaim his existence. Other than the John who has been merely imputed to the body and mind, there is no John. Thus, in this way we can see how we gain the view on the basis of the meditation: first we develop mental quiescence and next we proceed to analyze the nature of the subject.

For someone who has preceded his meditation on voidness with much study and training and has thus developed a strong predisposition towards this view, the actual realization that the self is devoid of inherent existence will come as a very joyful experience, like a poor man's discovery of a lot of money. But for those of us who have not acquired such a predisposition through previous inquiry, the realization that the I is merely imputed can be a very frightening experience. When we talk of the "fear of voidness," it is precisely this experience we are referring to.

When performing this investigation, the analytical aspect of the mind should start its search for the I at the top of the head and slowly and carefully proceed through the entire body down to the soles of the feet. In this way we shall realize that the self is not any of these physical parts and that none of these parts is the self; they are all merely parts of one's body. A similar analysis should then be made of the mind. Starting with visual consciousness we should proceed to investigate the other four sense consciousnesses and then the mental consciousness. Here too we shall find that no particular consciousness or aspect of consciousness is the self. Finally we should see if there is a self existing independently of the body and mind. It will be clear that once the body and mind have been withdrawn from the field of inquiry there can remain no possible grounds for determining the existence of a self. By means of these analyses we shall inevitably arrive at the conclusion that the I is something merely imputed to the body and mind and is devoid of any inherent existence.

There is the danger, however, that upon reading these descriptions of the merely-imputed self we shall construct a fixed idea of how such a self would appear to us and attempt to cognize it, thus creating an obstacle to our understanding the actual merely-imputed self. During the meditation it will be difficult to distinguish between our personal idea of the merely-imputed self and the actual merely-imputed self. The question will arise in our minds, "Does the self really exist in that way or have I simply imagined it to exist in that way?" Only through thorough and repeated meditative investigation shall we be able to solve this problem and achieve a valid perception of the I that is merely imputed to the body and mind.

It is quite possible that the following question may now arise. We have compared the self imputed to the body and mind to a snake imputed to a coil of rope and a person imputed to a pile of rocks. Now, although we imputed a snake and a person in this way, in reality they were utterly non-existent. Would it not follow, then, that although we impute the self to the body and mind, in fact the self does not exist at all? Such a conclusion would, of course, be absurd, because it is oneself who is meditating and making the analysis. To deny the self completely would be equivalent to denying that there is anyone meditating or investigating. Nevertheless, the *way* the I is imputed to the body and mind and the *way* the snake is imputed to the rope are identical. Furthermore, neither the I nor the snake exists inherently from its own side. The difference is that by imputing a snake to a rope we do not establish the existence of a snake whereas by imputing a self to the body and mind we do establish the existence of a self. This distinction between the non-existence of the snake and the existence of the self is possible because a rope is not a suitable basis upon which to impute a snake, whereas the body-mind complex is a suitable basis upon which to impute a self.

The aggregates of body and mind, either individually or collectively, are said to be a valid basis of imputation for the I, and the thought that imputes I to the aggregates is a conventionally valid mind. In dependence upon there being a valid basis of imputation and a conventionally valid imputing mind we are able to establish the existence of I, the self. Since this is the case we can correctly state "I am doing this" and "I am going there" without any contradiction. The I that is always thinking and acting exists.

Conversely, a coil of rope can never be a valid basis of imputation for a snake and therefore the thought that imputes a snake to it will always be an invalid and mistaken mind. A coil of rope, although it may be mistaken for a snake, will never be able to perform the function of a snake.

A correct process of imputation takes place in the following way. I see a friend of mine, Jack, coming down the road towards me. Strictly speaking, though, I see the physical form of Jack and then correctly impute Jack to it. Since Jack's form is a suitable basis of imputation for Jack, my imputation of Jack is valid and I can consequently state meaningfully that Jack is coming. Likewise, we say of ourselves, "I feel agitated today." Here we take this state of mind as the basis of imputation for ourselves. It too is a suitable basis and upon it we can correctly impute I. At death, however, our physical body ceases to act as a support for consciousness and perishes. At this time it can no longer serve as a valid basis of imputation for onself and neither can a valid thought that imputes oneself arise in reference to it.

Therefore, the existence of the self is established through the interdependent relationship between a valid basis of imputation and a valid imputing consciousness. In this way we say that the person exists, and this mode of existence we call "conventional," "nominal" or "apparent." The self exists in no way other than this. When, having followed this line of inquiry, we reach the understanding that the meditator is merely imputed upon his body and mind, then, upon observing a self that seems to exist in a way contrary to this — that is to say, inherently and substantially — we shall recognize the falsely-imagined self that is to be negated. In order to understand voidness it is extremely important to gain this recognition of the false I, because it is through realizing its absence that we come to understand voidness. When we discern the false self we become aware of the object of innate self-grasping, through whose force we are bound in cyclic existence. However, this is a very subtle point and before we can fully grasp its significance it is necessary to undertake much study, contemplation and repeated analytical investigation.

One common mistake made in this regard is to form one's own idea of what one thinks this false self must look like, hold this concept firmly in mind and thus proceed to negate it. In such a case, even if one vigorously applies all the various reasonings, the only thing one succeeds in doing is negating one's own personally fabricated false self. Consequently, one is no better off than when one started; the innate self-grasping will not have been in the least affected.

Generally speaking there are two principal ways to approach voidness: by understanding how things are mere conceptual imputations and thus inferring their void nature, and by realizing how they are dependent events and thus inferring their void nature. In this explanation of mahāmudrā we are following the first of those two methods. Just as we have examined the nature of the self and found it to be non-inherently existent and merely an imputation, likewise should we consider all other phenomena. At present, all phenomena appear to us falsely: everything appears to exist inherently, to exist objectively from its own side. For this reason we say that all our present states of consciousness are deceptive. Were we to free our minds from this deception we would realize that all phenomena that appear to us are not self-existent, concrete entities, but merely conceptual imputations. For us now, the way things appear does not correspond to the way they actually exist: they appear to us as inherently existent, whereas, in fact, they have not even the slightest trace of inherent existence. We assent to this fallacious appearance and subsequently conceive of phenomena as actually existing in that way. Upon this conceptual basis we proceed to crave for and become attached to objects that seem inherently pleasing and to develop aversion and hatred towards whatever appears to be inherently disagreeable. In this way we are led into all forms of emotional turmoil and mental unrest.

It is possible that we may object to the statement that all phenomena appear to us in a way in which they do not exist. Take an apple for example. We look at it and, on the basis of its appearance, are able to correctly identify it as an apple. Just as we expect, we are able to pick it up, eat it and find that it satisfies our hunger. To all intents and purposes it seems to exist in the way it appears. This of course is true and cannot be denied, but the point here is that we are deceived when we think that we are eating an apple that exists inherently from its own side. The apple we recognize, pick up and eat is only an imputedly-existent apple. *That* is the one that satisfies our hunger, not the inherently-existent one that appears to us.

This point might be made clearer by the following analogy. When someone is suffering from jaundice, not only does his skin turn yellow but, because the bile has affected his eyes, everything he sees appears yellowish. Say that this person decides to go skiing. Although the snow appears to be yellow, this does not hinder his ability to ski on it and make all forms of correct judgements about it. Likewise, phenomena falsely appear to be inherently existent, but this does not prevent us from making meaningful statements about them or from being able to predict their behaviour under certain conditions. However, as mentioned already, since our assenting to their false appearance leads us into all forms of dissatisfaction and suffering, to achieve genuine peace and liberation from bondage it is necessary that we recognize this false mode of appearance and realize it to be utterly non-existent. In this way we attain a perception of the voidness of the inherent existence of phenomena and thus realize their ultimate mode of existence. This is the understanding of mahāmudrā.

It is only when this insight is gained that we shall no longer be deceived by the way phenomena appear; we shall have eliminated the basis upon which we erroneously assented to inherent existence and became afflicted with attachment, hatred and so forth. Before we gain this insight it is like having an acquaintance who is always deceiving us. Until we are aware of his deceptions and the motives for his behaviour towards us, we shall continually be misled by his apparent friendship and honesty. When we understand that his speech and actions are not to be taken at face value but are merely a pretence, we shall respond in a way that will save us from his harmful intentions. Similarly, when we finally realize that phenomena do not exist as they appear, we shall be saved from all forms of frustration and despair. They will no longer be able to trick us into believing that they inherently exist.

The Buddha himself illustrated this mode of existence of

phenomena by certain well-chosen analogies. He compared phenomena to the illusory creations of magicians: although the magical horses and elephants conjured up by a magician appear to be real, in fact they are mere illusions produced by his magical spells and powers. Buddha also explained that life is similar to a dream. When we are fast asleep we might dream of a happy reunion with a friend, who later in the dream dies suddenly and we are overcome with grief. Although these events seem completely real and evoke the appropriate emotional reactions, when we wake up we realize that they did not really happen. In addition, he pointed out that things appear like the moon reflected in clear water: the reflection of the moon in a still lake is as clear as the moon in the sky. But if we reach out to touch it, our hand only disturbs the water, causing the reflection to disappear. Lastly, he said that existence is like a mirage. Travellers suffering from thirst in the desert often see an oasis of green trees and meadows in the distance, but as they get closer everything fades and disappears. Just as a magician's illusion, a dream, a reflection in water and a mirage do not exist as they appear, likewise all phenomena do not exist as they appear, i.e. as inherently existent. Nonetheless, they are not non-existent; they exist as mere conceptual imputations.

This completes what I have to say on mahāmudrā. However, here we have covered only some of the more essential points of the meditation; to deal with this subject in detail would require much more time.

Let us conclude with an episode from the life of Milarepa. While he was meditating, Milarepa was frequently disturbed by demons who tried to distract him from his practice. One time, as a means of banishing the demons from his cave, he arose from his meditation on mahāmudrā and shouted, "Be gone demons! I know now that you have no inherent existence." After a moment's reflection he added, "And neither do you, O Buddha."

Glossary

aggregates the various mental and physical constituents of conditioned existence, specifically of the person.

apperception the aspect of consciousness that is aware only of the consciousness itself. It is asserted by the Chittamātra school and refuted by the Mādhyamaka school.

arhat one who has achieved liberation from cyclic existence: the goal of the Hinayāna practitioner.

attachment the deluded mental factor that is attracted to and wishes to possess misery-producing objects, mistakenly believing them to be true sources of happiness.

aversion the deluded mental factor that seeks to be separated from and generates anger towards unpleasant objects.

Avalokiteshvara the bodhisattva embodying the boundless compassion of full enlightenment.

bodhisattva a Mahāyāna practitioner; someone striving to gain the full enlightenment of buddhahood in order to benefit others.

buddha one who has removed every gross and subtle obscuration veiling the mind and has developed all good qualities, such as wisdom, compassion and skilful means, to the full.

buddhahood full enlightenment: the goal of the Mahāyāna practitioner.

Chandrakīrti Indian master of the sixth century who elucidated Nagarjuna's exposition of the Mādhyamaka philosophy; author of the *Mādhyamakāvtāra*.

Chārvāka a non-Buddhist school of materialist thinkers who denied the validity of the law of moral causation (karma).

Chittamātra third of the four major schools of Buddhist philosophy; this Mahāyāna school denies the existence of external objects and asserts the true existence of the mind; sometimes referred to as the Mind-only school.

cyclic existence Skt., samsara; the unsatisfactory state of existence, rooted in ignorance of the actual nature of reality, in which beings experience the various sufferings of repeated death and rebirth.

dependent arising the dependent and relational character of phenomena; any phenomenon so characterized. Establishing things as dependent arisings — i.e. as dependent upon parts, causes and mental imputation for their existence — overcomes the false view of their being inherently self-existent.

dharmakāya the unobscured, omniscient mind of a buddha; the truth body.

enlightenment the state of realization of an arhat or a buddha.

existence

    conventional existence the interdependent nature of phenomena; their manner of appearance and functioning.

    inherent existence the falsely conceived way in which phenomena are believed to exist, i.e. without depending upon parts, causes and mental imputation.

foundation consciousness Skt., *ālayavijñāna*; asserted by the Chittamātra school as the consciousness upon which the seeds of karmic actions are placed.

four formless absorptions states of deep meditative concentration

four immeasurables meditation upon love, compassion, equanimity and joyfulness.

Gelug one of the four major Tibetan traditions of Buddhism, established in the fifteenth century by Je Tsong Khapa and his followers.

geshe title conferred on one who has completed a Tibetan

monastic education in such Buddhist studies as logic, epistemology, philosophy, metaphysics and rules of discipline.

guru   spiritual mentor and guide

Hinayāna   those paths of Buddhist thought and practice stressing the attainment of individual or self-liberation from the sufferings of cyclic existence; the so-called lesser vehicle.

ignorance   unknowing; specifically the deluded mental factor that is mistaken about the actual way in which things exist; the root of cyclic existence and all suffering.

impute   designate; apprehend; the mental process by which phenomena are established to exist conventionally.

karma   intentional action that determines the nature of future experience in accordance with the laws or moral causation.

Mādhyamaka   a school of Buddhist philosophy formulated by Nāgārjuna, Chandrakīrti and others on the basis of the *Perfection of Wisdom (prajñāpāramitā) Sutras* of the Buddha. It emphasizes the voidness of all phenomena through a radical denial of any notions such as substance, essence, and inherent existence. Through understanding voidness one is freed from the ignorance that keeps one bound to samsara.

Mahāyāna   those paths of Buddhist thought and practice stressing the attainments of the full enlightenment of buddhahood for the benefit of others; the paths of the bodhisattva; the so-called greater vehicle.

mandala   a circular diagram symbolic of the universe; the visualized abode of a meditational deity.

mantra   Sanskrit syllables and words used in tantric practices to transform ordinary speech and protect the mind from ordinary conceptualizations.

method   those practices of compassion and so forth leading to the attainment of the form body (*rūpakāya*) of a buddha.

Mount Meru   the hub around which the various segments of the universe are arranged; visualized especially at the centre of mandala offerings.

Nāgārjuna   Indian Buddhist master of the second century who elucidated the *Perfection of Wisdom Sutras* of Buddha; the major expounder of the Mādhyamaka philosophy.

name-mantra of guru Sanskrit syllables incorporating the name of one's spiritual mentor, recited to enhance devotion and to request inspiration.

nirmanakāya the form in which a buddha appears to ordinary beings; the emanation body.

nirvana liberation from cyclic existence; the "higher" nirvana refers to the complete enlightenment of a buddha.

pratyekabuddha solitary realizer; a Hinayana practitioner who does not rely on a spiritual master during the final stages of the path.

qualities (*sattva, rajah, tamah*) asserted by the non-Buddhist Sāṃkhya school as the three basic constituents of the "primal substance" (*prakrti*): lightness, activity and darkness.

rūpakāya the form body of a buddha comprising the sambhogakāya and nirmanakāya.

sambogakāya the form in which a buddha appears to advanced bodhisattvas; the enjoyment body.

Sāṃkhya Enumerator; a non-Buddhist school asserting twenty-five categories of objects of knowledge.

Sammitaya one of the eighteen earliest schools of Buddhism; classified by the Tibetans as one of the sub-sects of the Vaibāṣhika school.

samsara cyclic existence

Saraha Indian master; mentor to Nagarjuna and highly accomplished tantric practitioner.

Shākyamuni title conferred upon Gautama Buddha (sixth century BC); Sage of the Shākya Clan.

Shāriputra one of Shākyamuni's closest disciples, known for his wisdom.

shrāvaka hearer; a Hinayāna practitioner who relies on a spiritual master throughout his training.

shūnyatā voidness; emptiness; the absence of inherent existence; the ultimate mode of being of all phenomena.

sutra a discourse preached by the Buddha; the non-tantric way to enlightenment.

tantra an esoteric discource attributed to the Buddha; a way to enlightenment which makes use of mantra, visualization, and the control of subtle physical energies; the adamantine vehicle to enlightenment (vajrayana).

ten bhumis   the ten stages or grounds through which advanced bodhisattvas pass on their way to enlightenment.

ten powers of a buddha   (1) the power of knowing right from wrong; (2) the power of knowing the consequences of actions; (3) the power of knowing the various inclinations of living beings; (4) the power of knowing the various types of living beings; (5) the power of knowing the degree of the capacities of living beings; (6) the power of knowing the path that leads everywhere; (7) the power of knowing the obscurations, afflictions and purifications of all contemplations, meditations, liberations, concentrations and absorptions; (8) the power of knowing one's former lives; (9) the power of knowing the time of death and future lives; (10) the power of knowing the exhaustion of defilements. (Adapted from Thurman, Robert, *The Holy Teachings of Virmalakirti.* Pennsylvania State University Press, 1976.)

Tsong Khapa   founder of the Gelug tradition of Tibetan Buddhism.

twelve links   the twelvefold chain of causation describing the way in which suffering arises from ignorance and the actions motivated by ignorance; (1) ignorance; (2) formative actions; (3) consciousness; (4) name and form; (5) the six sense bases; (6) contact; (7) feeling; (8) craving; (9) longing; (10) existence; (11) birth; (12) ageing and death.

two truths   conventional or deceptive truth, i.e. the way in which phenomena normally appear and function, and ultimate truth, i.e. the way in which phenomena actually exist.

Vaishesika   Particularist; a non-Buddhist school teaching a path to liberation employing ablutions, fasts, etc.

view of the transitory composite   the mistaken view with which one believes one's I or self to exist independently and inherently, instead of being a mere imputation on the ever-changing aggregates.

voidness   shunyata

wisdom   knowing or understanding, specifically of the actual way in which things exist; the realizations leading to the attainment of the truth body (*dharmakāya*) of a buddha.

yogī   a practitioner following a spiritual discipline that "yokes" him or her to a specific path and practice; one who has mastered the practices of concentration and insight.

yidam   a meditational deity visualized and invoked in tantric practices with whom the practitioner learns to identify.

Bibliography

(The references for the entries marked 'P' are to the Peking edition of the Tibetan Tripiṭaka published by the Suzuki Research Foundation, Tokyo-Kyoto, 1956.)

Buddha. *Confession Sutra, Triskandhanāmamahāyānasūtra, phung.po.gsum.po'i.mdo.* P.950, vol. 37. Trans. B. Beresford, in *Mahāyāna Purification Practices.* Dharamsala: Library of Tibetan Works and Archives, 1978.

————*Descent into Lanka Sutra, Laṅkāvatārasūtra, lang.kar. gshegs.pa'i.mdo.* P.775 vol. 29. Trans. D.T. Suzuki, *The Laṅkāvatāra Sūtra.* London: Routledge and Kegan Paul, 1973.

————*Eight Thousand Stanza Perfection of Wisdom Sutra, Aṣṭasāhasrikāprajñāpāramitāsūtra, shes.rab.kyi.pha.rol.tu. phyin.pa.brgyad.stong.pa'i.mdo.* P.734 vol. 21. Trans. Edward Conze, *The Perfection of Wisdom in Eight Thousand Lines and its Verse Summary.* Bolinas, Four Seasons Foundation, 1973.

————*The Heart of Wisdom, Bhagavatiprajñāpāramitāsū-trapañcāshikā, bcom.ldan.mdas.ma.shes.rab.kyi.pha.rol.tu. phyin.pa'i.mdo.lnga.bcu.pa.* P.740 vol. 21.

————*Hundred Thousand Stanza Perfection of Wisdom Sūtra, Shatasāhasrikāprajñāpāramitāsūtra, shes.rab.kyi.pha.rol.tu.*

phyin.pa.stong.phrag.brgya.pa. P.730 vol. 12-18. Trans. Edward Conze, *The Large Sutra on Perfect Wisdom.* Berkeley: University of California Press, 1975.

———*Meeting of Father and Son Sutra, Pitāputrasamāgamasūtra, yab.dang.sras.mjal.ba'i.mdo.* P.760.16, vol. 23.

———*Relieving the Remorse of Ajātashatra Sutra, Ajātashatrakaukṛtyavinodanāsūtra, ma.skyes.dgra'i.'gyod.pa.bsal.ba'i.mdo.* P.882, vol. 35.

———*The Ten Dharmas Sutra, Dashadharmakasūtra, chos.bcu. pa'i.mdo.* P.760.9 vol. 22.

———*Twenty Five Thousand Stanza Perfection of Wisdom Sutra, Pañcaviṃshatisāhasrikāprajñāpāramitāsūtra, shes.rab.kyi.pha. rol.tu.phyin.pa.stong.phrag.nyi.shu.lnga.pa.* P.731, vol. 18-19.

Chandrakīrti. *Commentary to 'A Guide to the Middle Way', Mādhyamakāvatārabhāṣya, dbu.ma.la.'jug.pa'i.bshad. pa.* P.5263, vol. 98.

———*A Guide to the Middle Way, Mādhyamakāvatāra, dbu.ma.la.jug.pa.* P.5261 and 5262, vol. 98.

Dül-nag-pa Päl-dän. *The Hundreds of Deities of the Land of Joy. dga'.ldan.lha.brgya.ma.* Trans. Alexander Berzin, Dharamsala: Library of Tibetan Works and Archives, 1979.

Gyatso, Tenzin, the XIV Dalai Lama, *The Inseparability of the Spiritual Master and Avalokiteshvara, bla.ma.dang.spyan.ras. gzigs.dbyer.med.kyi.rnal.'byor.dngos.grub.kun.'byung.* Trans. Sherpa Tulku, Dharamsala: Library of Tibetan Works and Archives, 1975.

Maitreya. *The Ornament of Clear Realization, Abhisamayālaṃkāra, mngon.par.rtogs.pa'i.rgyan.* P.5184, vol. 88.

Nāgārjuna. *Fundamental Stanzas on the Middle Way, Prajñānāmamūlamādhyamakakārikā, dbu.ma.rtsa.ba'i.tshig. le'ur.byas.pa.shes.rab.ces.bya.ba.* P.5224, vol. 95. Trans. Kenneth K. Inada, *Nāgārjuna: Mūlamādhyamakakārikā.* Tokyo: Hokuseido Press, 1970.

Panchen Losang Chö-kyi-Gyaltsen. *The Lamp of Clear Illumination: an Extensive Commentary to the Root Text for the Gelugpa Oral Tradition of Mahāmudrā, dge.ldan.bka'.brgyud. rin.po.che'i.bka.srol.phyag.rgya.chen.po'i.rtsa.ba.rgyas.*

par.bshad.pa.yang.gsal.sgron.me. Blockprint in the Possession of Geshé Rabten, date unknown.

————*Root Text for the Gelugpa Oral Tradition of Mahāmudrā*, *dge.ldan.bka'.brgyud.rin.po.che'i.phyag.chen.rtsa.ba.rgyal. ba'i.gzhung.lam*. Trans. with oral commentary Geshe Ngawang Dargyey et alia, *The Great Seal of Voidness*. Dharamsala: Library of Tibetan Works and Archives, 1975.

Shāntideva. *A Guide to the Bodhisattva's Way of Life*, *Bodhisattvacharyāvatāra*, *(byang.chub.sems.dpa'i.spyod.pa. la.'jug.pa.)* P.5272, vol. 99. Trans. Stephen Batchelor, Dharamsala: Library of Tibetan Works and Archives, 1979.

Tsong Khapa. *Clear Illumination of the Intention, bstan.bcos.chen. po.dbu.ma.la.'jug.pa'i.rnam.bshad.dgongs.pa.rab.gsal*. P.6143, vol. 154.

Suggested Additional Reading

Conze, Edward. *The Short Prajñāpāramitā Texts*. London: Luzac and Co., 1973.

Guenther, H.V. *Mahāmudrā — The Method of Self-Actualization*. The Tibet Journal, vol.1, no.1, p.5. Dharamsala: Library of Tibetan Works and Archives, 1975.

Gyatso, Kelsang, Geshe. *Clear Light of Bliss*. Trans. Tenzin Norbu, ed. Jonathan Landaw, London: Wisdom Publications, 1982.

————*Meaningful to Behold*. Trans. Tenzin Norbu, ed. Jonathan Landaw, London: Wisdom Publications, 1980.

Gyatso, Tenzin, the XIV Dalai Lama. *The Buddhism of Tibet and the Key to the Middle Way*. Trans. Jeffrey Hopkins, London: George Allen and Unwin, 1975.

Hopkins, Jeffrey. *Meditation on Emptiness*. London: Wisdom Publications, 1983.

McDonald, Kathleen. *Basic Buddhist Meditations*. London: Wisdom Publications, 1983.

Sopa, Lhundup, Geshe, and Hopkins, Jeffrey. *Practice and Theory of Tibetan Buddhism*. London: Rider, 1976.

Wangchug Dorje, the IX Karmapa. *The Mahāmudrā Eliminating*

the Darkness of Ignorance, with commentary by Beru Khyentse Rinpoche. Trans. Alexander Berzin, Dharamsala: Library of Tibetan Works and Archives, 1978.

Other Works by Geshé Rabten

Advice from a Spiritual Friend, (with Geshe Ngawang Dargyey). Trans. Gonsar Tulku, ed. B. Beresford, London: Wisdom Publications, 1983. (Reprint)

The Graduated Path to Liberation. Tr. Gonsar Tulku, Delhi: Mahayana Publications, 1982 (first edition: Cambridge, England, 1972). (Reprint)

The Life and Teachings of Geshé Rabten. Trans. and ed. B. Alan Wallace, London: George, Allen and Unwin, 1980.

Mahāmudrā. Trans and ed. Gonsar Tulku, Brian Beresford and Stephen Batchelor, Zürich: Theseus Verlag, 1979 (German language edition).

The Mind and its Functions. Trans. and ed. Stephen Batchelor, Tharpa Choeling: 1978.

The Preliminary Practices. Trans. Gonsar Tulku, ed. Georges Driessens, Dharamsala: Library of Tibetan Works and Archives, 1974 (revised ed. 1976).